PORTON
A DEADLY TRAP

The Facts about the Battle of Porton Plantation
BOUGAINVILLE 1945
by
Audrey Davidson
and
Battle Survivors

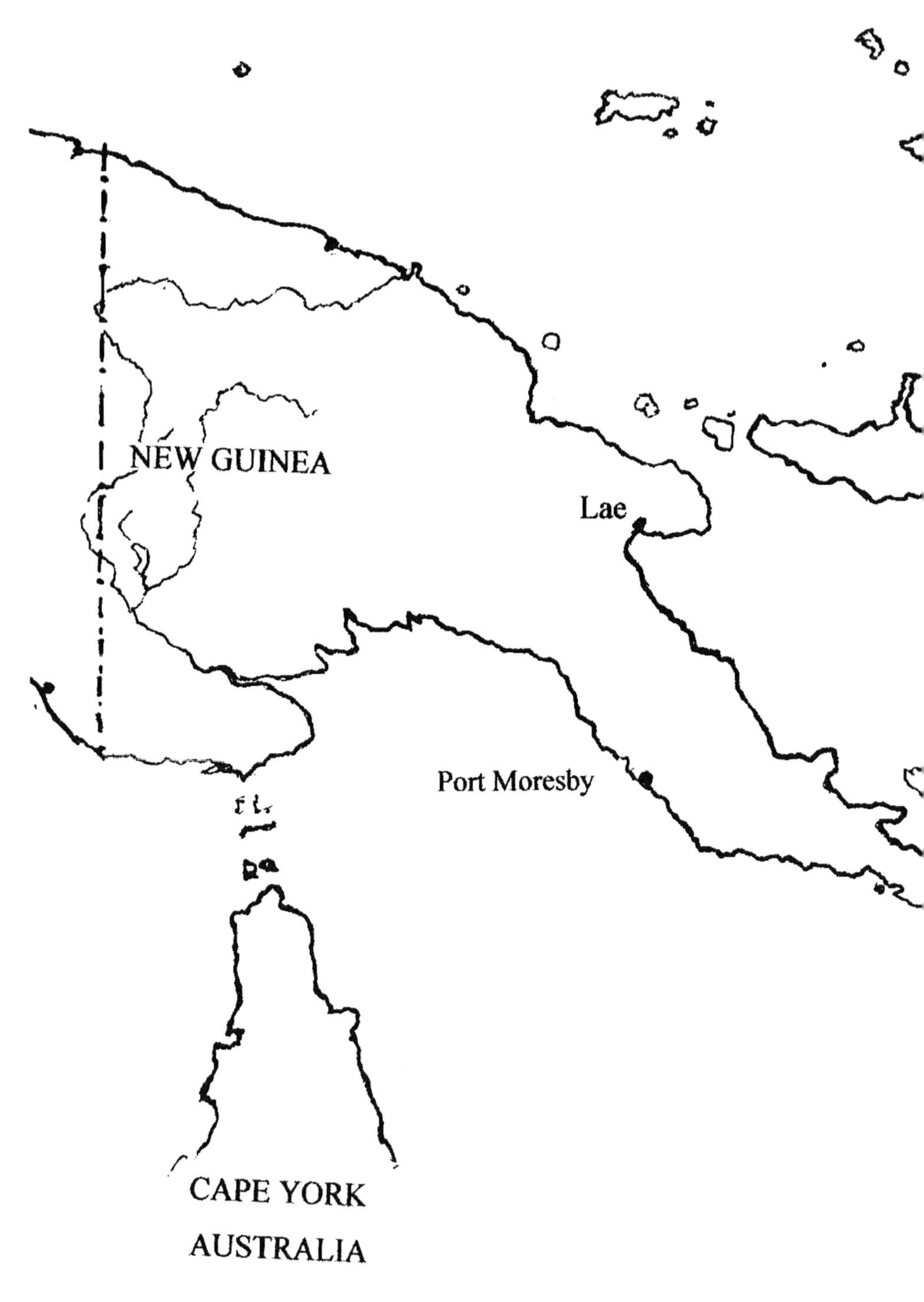
NEW GUINEA
Lae
Port Moresby
CAPE YORK
AUSTRALIA

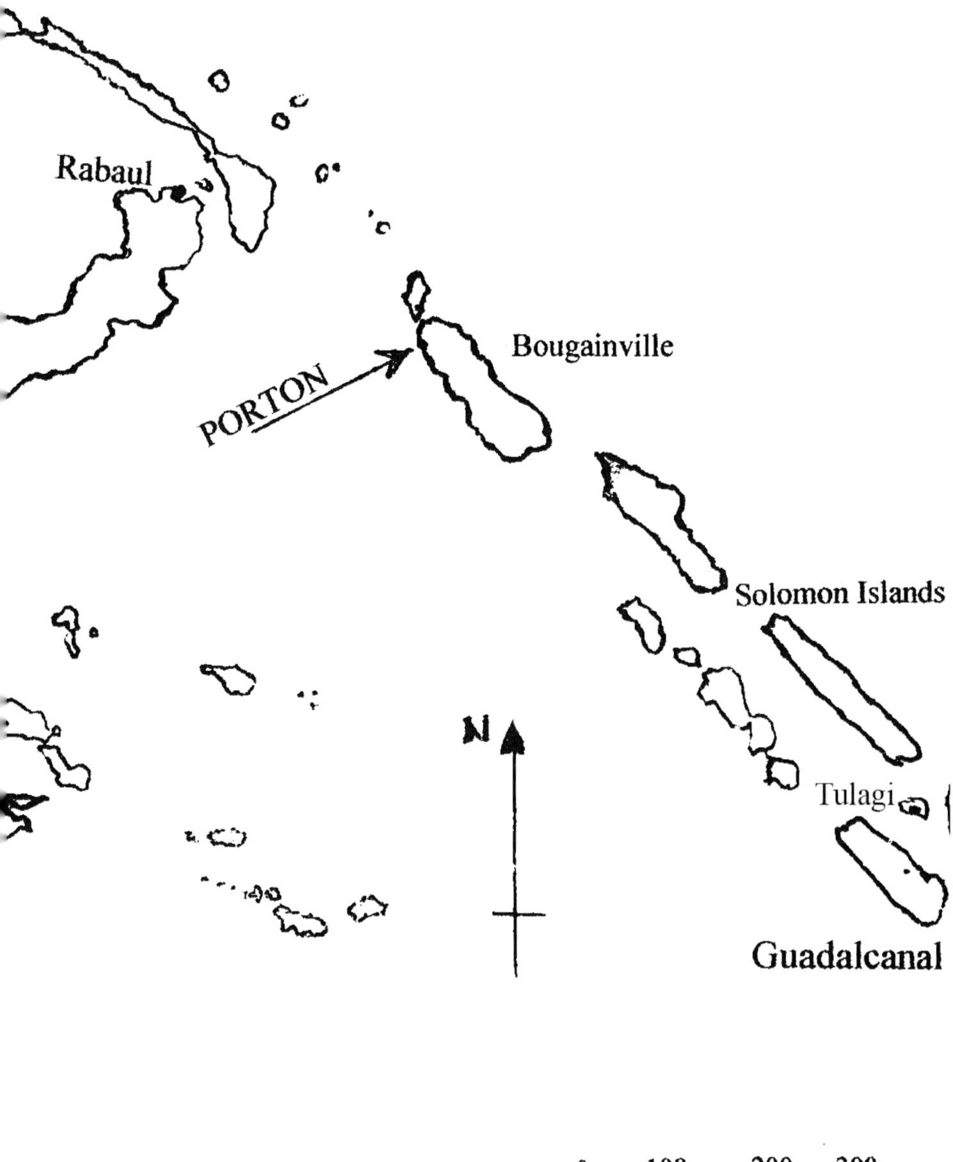

Rabaul
Bougainville
PORTON
Solomon Islands
N
Tulagi
Guadalcanal
0
100
200
300
kilometres

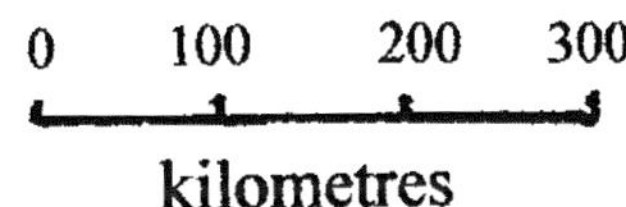

First published in 2005 by Boolarong Press
Copyright © Audrey Davidson

This book is copyright. Apart from any fair dealing for the purpose of private study, research, criticism or review, as permitted under the Copyright Act, no part may be reproduced by any process without written permission. Inquiries should be addressed to the Publishers.

The author wishes to acknowledge the support of the Australian Government Department of Veterans' Affairs, which provided a grant to assist publication under the Australian Government's commemorations program, *Saluting Their Service.*

The Department has not participated in the research or production or exercised editorial control over the work's contents, and the views expressed and conclusions reached herein do not not necessarily represent those of the commmonwealth, which expressly disclaims any responsibility for the content or accuracy of the work.

All rights reserved.

National Library of Australia
Cataloguing-in-Publication data

Davidson, Audrey., - .
Porton A Deadly Trap: The Battle that Vanished,

ISBN 0-646-44766-1

BOOLARONG PRESS
35 Hamilton Road, Moorooka, Brisbane, Qld 4105
Printed and Bound by Watson Ferguson & Co.
Moorooka 4105

PROUDLY PRINTED IN QUEENSLAND

Cover: Colin Peck

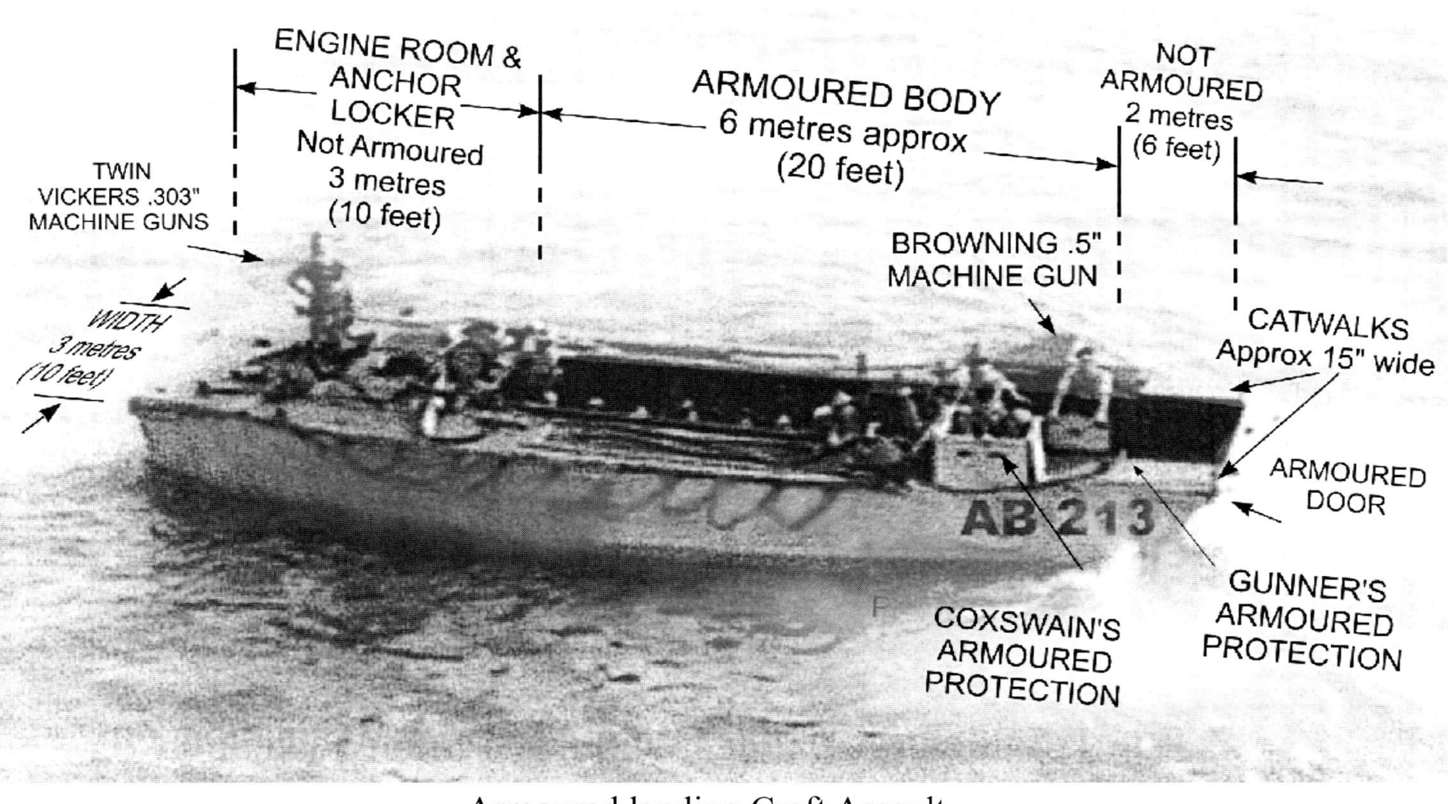

Armoured landing Craft Assault

Capt. Clyde Downs June 1945, Bougainville.

Dedication

I dedicate this book to all the brave men who fought at Porton, many of whom, like my father Capt. Clyde Downs, paid the supreme sacrifice in a battle they knew would be in vain.

Foreword

In July 2003 Audrey Davidson gave a video presentation and address to an 11 Brigade Reunion Luncheon in Brisbane. Her film featured the cathartic visit she had made some months earlier to a beach near Soraken in North Bougainville around which the WWII Battle of Porton Plantation had raged during the fateful hours of June 8-10 1945. Her father, Captain Clyde Downs who commanded the 31st/51st Australian Infantry Battalion attack force, was killed in action. His body was never found.

The Battle of Porton was well-known to Audrey's audience but the depth of the response to her pictures and words that day surprised her; were there tales untold behind the quiet pride of the self-effacing survivors who came up to speak to her afterwards? Audrey resolved to find out before it was too late; she would ask each and every Porton veteran to allow her to "see" the battle through his eyes and then weave these remarkable stories into the first "from the heart" account of an action during which mateship and steadfast courage under fire were the norm.

Somewhere along the way, I suspect, Audrey Davidson became a privileged "daughter of the regiment", and this book a daughter's ultimate homage, first and foremost to the father she cherished and lost to war, and then to those of his comrades-in-arms who were killed, wounded, or lost in action during that nightmarish encounter. In doing so she has given the Battle of Porton and those who took part in it their rightful place among the nation's most compelling tales of military heroism.

SJ (John) Gardner, MBE, ED,
(formerly 31st Battalion, The
Royal Queensland Regiment).

Acknowledgments

I sincerely thank the Department of Veteran Affairs for their SalutingTheir Service Commemorations grant which has made this publication achievable. I also thank the Australian War Memorial for their helpful advice and their permission to reproduce appropriate photographs.

I am grateful to Major General John Pearn, Patron of the Australian Water Transport Association (Qld), who offered me the challenge of writing this story which is very close to my heart – knowing that I had no experience as an historian but trusting that my credentials, as the daughter of a Porton soldier, were sufficient for the task.

I also wish to thank Lieutenant Colonel D. Moffett, ex-C.O. 31st Infantry Battalion, who kindly edited the early draft of this book and offered me welcome advice on military matters and protocol.

I take this opportunity to thank my family and friends who have helped and supported me during the writing of the book, who had faith in my ability to finish this complex project which in the beginning seemed so simple!

Special thanks must go to my army of co-authors – the real authors without whom there would be no book – the survivors. Their revealing eye-witness accounts appear for the first time in this volume. I am grateful to those vets who also gave their time for interviews and all-important oral histories, and to those who sent me their treasured old war-time photographs.

I am deeply indebted to 11th Brigade war hero and Porton survivor, Captain Blue Reiter, M.C. M.M. M.I.D. He is a friend who has generously shared with me his personal account of the operation as well as relevant

Intelligence reports, official records, the Unit diary, maps and documents which have been indispensable in putting this history together. I have benefited from his cheerful support and guidance especially in regard to Army matters and procedures.

I also acknowledge my debt to journalist and documentary-maker Murray McCloskey for his unstinting support and his permission to use some transcripts from the T.V. documentary The Savage Shore; to my friend John Gardner M.B.E., author of the Life and Times series of Army biographies, and editor of the Whispering Boomerang (news bulletin of the 31st Infantry Battalion), for his help and the Introduction to this book and for valuable information regarding Battalion history and personnel; to Lionel Veale, author of the pre-war and war-time missions of the No.1 Independent Company of commandos and Coastwatchers in New Guinea and the Solomons, for his encouragement and research material on Bougainville; to artists and friends Marilyn and Colin Peck for their professional help with the cover design, and for Col's inspired computer imaging.

I thank Peter Taylor, historian and ex-publisher, for his editing and advice on the structure of this book. His text directions and corrections have been much appreciated. Any errors which remain are mine alone.

I am grateful to the 11th Brigade for their encouragement, and also to Major Bill Hughes M.B.E. for his comprehensive book on the history of the 31st/51st Battalion which I have relied upon heavily for research material. I thank Len Flynn for his copy of this book which is now out of print.

Last but foremost I acknowledge the debt I owe my dear and long-suffering husband Peter who has given me welcome assistance at every stage of this book – journeying north and south and west to meet the Porton vets, copying, mapping, editing, proof-reading, advising, suggesting changes which I have sometimes been happy to include. He has borne the tears and tantrums and takeaways with great fortitude and I thank him most sincerely.

Porton Beach from the sea

Who Are These Men?

Who are these men who march so proud
Who quietly weep, eyes closed, head bowed?
These are the men who once were boys
Who missed out on youth with all of its joys

Who are these men with aged faces
Who silently count the empty spaces?
These are the men who gave their all
Who fought for their country for freedom for all.

Who were these men with sorrowful look
Who still can remember the lives that were took?
These are the men who saw young men die
The price of peace is always high.

Who are these men who promise to keep
Alive in their hearts the one God holds asleep?
These are the men to whom I promise again
Veterans, my friends, I will remember them.

By Jodie Johnson (aged 11)
Lancashire, England.

Contents

Prologue

This is the story of the Battle of Porton Plantation on Bougainville Island in 1945. It is a story which should and must be told, examined, and understood for what it is - a record of the blighted lives and hopes of a small group of Australian servicemen, brought about by official incompetence and a powerful man's overriding ambition. It is not till the body of evidence is publicly viewed and then given a decent burial that the grieving and healing processes can begin for the remaining survivors of that tragic conflict. These ageing men will then be able to feel that the ordeal they endured together so long ago has at last been acknowledged and recognised – that belated homage has been paid to the mates they lost so needlessly on Porton beach.

The main object in writing the story is not to dwell unduly upon the horrors of that conflict, or on apportioning blame where it most obviously lies – the records most amply illustrate our criticisms. The object is to give those men who fought at Porton in 1945 a voice after almost sixty years of silence, so that they can tell their story and might then be able to put the pain and anguish of that battle behind them. So they can be assured that the world will know how and why it can happen that good and loyal men are forced into the deplorable situation where they must fight and die for no reason but the ineptitude of some senior officers and the aggrandisement and advancement of another.

I did not go looking for this story; it found me. I realize now that it had been stalking me in the shadows since 1945 – since my father was reported missing in action at Porton Plantation on June 10 of that year. It seemed obvious to me then, as a child, that if Dad was missing someone should be out there seriously trying to find him. But he was never found. It was in 2002, fifty-seven years later, that with some difficulty and with much help from the Defence Department and the Department of Veteran Affairs, I was able to make my own visit to that forgotten and lonely battlefield at Porton.

After returning from Bougainville I reported back to my father's old Battalion and, at their 11th Brigade Reunion in Brisbane in 2002, I showed them a short video of Porton beach as it looks to-day. It was suggested by the veterans at that time that I write the story of the battle. Being no historian, and knowing nothing of the mysteries of weaponry or field-craft or the life of servicemen in the field, I quickly realised there was only one way to succeed with this project. That was, of course, to appeal to the experts – the men who were there doing the fighting in 1945, the survivors themselves.

I asked them for their stories. They responded magnificently with moving accounts of their experiences - some hauntingly personal. There were old photographs – of planes, now-obsolete landing barges, coconut palms, the blasted and desolate beach, wounded men on a hospital barge and military top brass stepping out of aeroplanes or conferring over large maps. These pictures had been taken by official war photographers. The others - the faded snapshots showing laughing, vital, carefree young men and boys in crumpled soldiers' uniforms – were personal. These young men had yet to be tested at Porton.

The old Diggers also gave me their maps, the Battalion Confidential Report, Intelligence Report and the Unit Diary. It was obvious that the events they recalled in their stories were deeply etched and still vivid in their memories. Though unimportant details sometimes differed in the telling by some of the men, the essential core of their experiences was chillingly consistent. As I read, there were times when I felt like a trespasser on their private grief as they described the loss of their mates and the unimaginable privation they endured during those three days of hell.

Some of the men found their battle memories too painful to commit to paper. I am grateful for the time they found to just sit and talk to me – at times a little emotionally – about Porton. Their oral histories were rich in background detail, and some privileged glimpses were permitted into the lives and thoughts of these fighting men in action.

However, by far the strongest message to come from the stories was the survivors' underlying feeling of betrayal, of knowing well that the battle they had been sent to fight was altogether pointless; and of knowing that the horrific conditions they endured could have been avoided with good planning and control by military strategists at the upper level of command. There was also anger from many that their ordeal at Porton had never been recognised and made public for reasons that appeared to be wholly political.

To address those concerns the survivors have now, for the first time, been given a chance to be heard. Their testimonies, together with the records contained in the 31st/51st Battalion's Confidential Report (written by the Intelligence Officer on July 9 1945), the Unit Diary, and Gavin Long's official documentation in *Australia in the War 39 – 45, Vol. vii, The Final Campaigns* contain the story of the Porton battle. My task is to make that story known. It is a responsibility, a gift and a privilege to write this book.

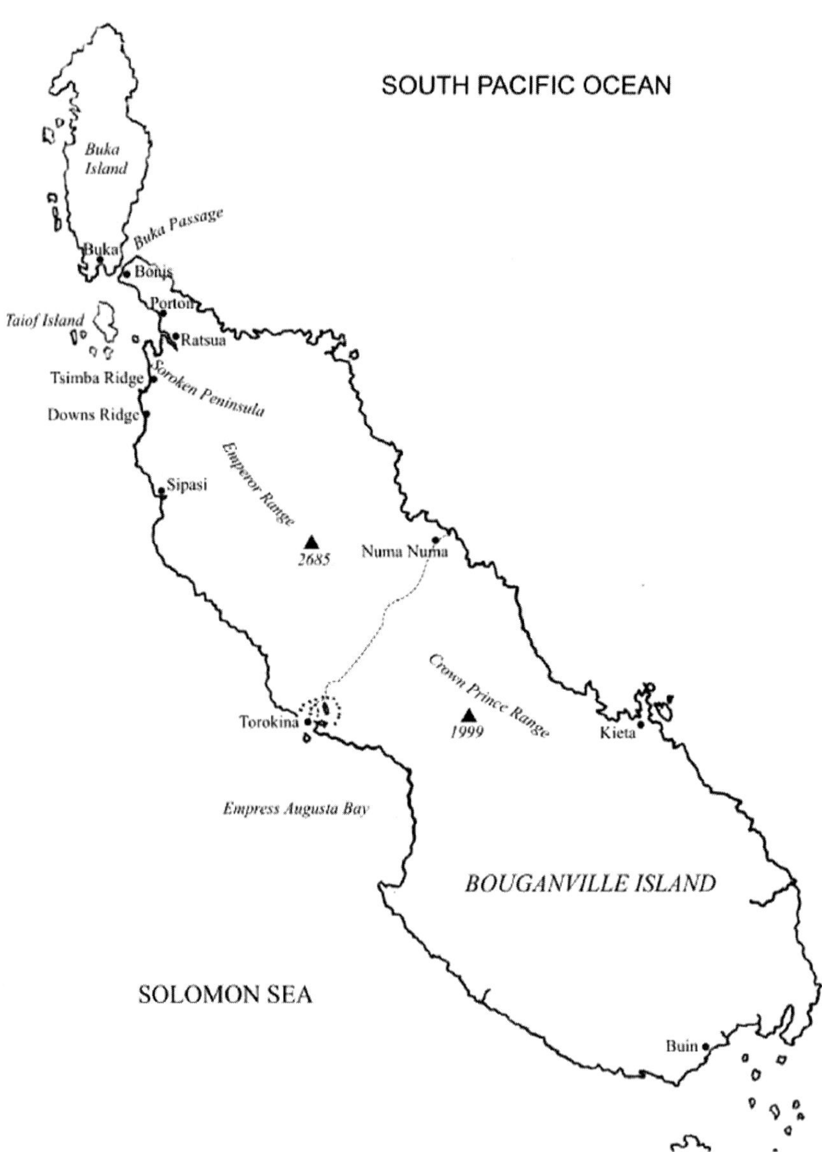
SOUTH PACIFIC OCEAN
Buka Island
Buka Passage
Buka
Bonis
Porton
Taiof Island
Ratsua
Tsimba Ridge
Soroken Peninsula
Downs Ridge
Emperor Range
Sipasi
2685
Numa Numa
Crown Prince Range
Torokina
1999
Kieta
Empress Augusta Bay
BOUGANVILLE ISLAND
SOLOMON SEA
Buin

The Battleground 1

"PORTON": a Name, a Beach, a Plantation, a Battle a Betrayal, a Bitter Memory

Porton is a name which can still strike dread into the hearts of men. A handful of elderly veterans remember the beach at Porton Plantation on the island of Bougainville. In June 1945 they survived the brief but bloody offensive which took place there eight weeks before the end of WWII. Some of those diggers are still fighting that old battle.

The men were driven to the limit of endurance on Porton beach. During three terrible days of fighting there they were forced to witness many of their mates being needlessly killed or wounded by Japanese gunfire in an operation which was known to be both pointless and unwarranted. The full facts were never revealed and the survivors have bitter memories.

The offensives in the south west Pacific in WWII were fought mostly on hot, steamy, jungle-clad islands. The battlefields on Bougainville were no exception. This was wild and dangerous terrain and the troops were required to undergo rigorous jungle warfare training in Australia prior to embarkation for the Pacific.

The islands of Bougainville and Buka form part of the Solomon Islands group, a chain of islands which is separated from Australia by the Coral Sea:

> 'These two islands are separated by a narrow passage approximately 800 metres wide. Through the passage a vicious current rips at about 12 knots, so strong that those crossing by canoe were often carried 800 metres off course before reaching the other side. Buka Island is 50 kilometres long and 20 kilometres wide. The highest point, Mt.

Popagen, is about 400 metres high.'[1]

Deceptively beautiful, Bougainville is one of the most northerly, and the largest, of these Solomon Islands, measuring approximately 180 kilometres in length and 64 kilometres at its widest point. It reposes seductively in a turquoise sea behind ramparts of encircling coral reefs and the luxuriant tropical vegetation and volcanic cloud-topped mountains (Mt. Balbi rises to 2600 metres) are the stuff of to-day's colourful tourist brochures. The island has the appearance of the perfect tropical paradise.

However, the narrow flat coastal shelf is not an ideal tourist location. There are many tidal rivers and estuaries here and almost impenetrable mangrove swamps bring a multitude of health problems in the steamy equatorial climate. This was inhospitable territory for the servicemen, Allied and Japanese alike, who fought in the Bougainville campaigns during World War 11.

The troops were not only fighting the enemy, the heat, the rampant vegetation, mosquitoes and incessant torrential rain, they were also fighting disease. While malaria, dengue fever and dysentery daily took their grim toll, tropical ulcers, fungal and pernicious skin infections and parasitic infestations often added greatly to the suffering. Of the actual 30,000 – 40,000 Japanese on Bougainville at that time, approximately 10,000 were thought to have died from disease and starvation – 'the "vicious" tropical diseases and malnutrition, much more dreadful then bullets, from which we suffered most.'[3]

[1] *We Were the First. Unit History of the No.1 Independent Company,* Alexander McNab, Australian Military History Publications, 1998, p86.

[3]Letter from Sub Lieutenant Genna Katsumata to John Feltham.

The narrow Bonis Peninsula forms the northern extremity of Bougainville, and is adjacent to Buka Passage. The Japanese occupied Buka in 1942 and built an important air strip and garrison there. This close proximity to the Bougainville mainland allowed for the quick transit of their troops and supplies from Buka to Bonis after the Australian assault force landed at Porton in 1945.[4]

The details which follow appear in Major W.E. Hughes' history of the 31st/51st Battalion.[5]

Porton coconut plantation, backed by jungle and minor ridges to the east, is situated in an area of coral swamps on the west coast of Bonis Peninsula. It nestles at the edge of Matchin Bay, a small horseshoe-shaped inlet in which lie several islands, brilliant green brushstrokes against the blue water of the bay. Saposa, Taiof, and Torokori Islands were all important during the course of the Porton battle.

Porton's narrow gently-sloping beach is lined with driftwood and coarse secondary growth with large stands of wild banana groves. Rampant kunai grass and coconut palms crowd almost to the water's edge. In the background towers the solid dark wall of the surrounding jungle. The protecting reef appears innocent enough beneath the translucent green water of the shallows. However, there is only one safe deep-water channel to be found through this reef. It provides the sole access from the sea to the plantation's jetty. The passage is narrow, requiring both local knowledge and skilful navigation to negotiate successfully. Bombing by the American Air Force rendered the jetty unserviceable in 1944.

[4] *"At War with the 31/51st Infantry Battalion",* Major W.E. Hughes MBE RL, Church Archivist Press, 1993, p203.

[5] Ibid.

Chabai village and Tarlena Mission, where the Japanese stationed themselves in 1942, are situated a short distance to the north of Porton beach. Soraken Peninsula, visible 8 kilometres away to the south, was where the Australian 4th Field Regiment sited its No 12 battery of "25 pounders" during the Porton battle in 1945. The 11th Brigade Headquarters and forward bases were on "F"[Freddie] Beach and "I" Beach, approximately 6 kilometres south of Soraken Peninsula at the mouth of the Compton River.

It was learned later from captured Japanese documents that, from a tree-top lookout on Buka Island 40 kilometres away, the enemy were able to observe Allied troop movements on Soraken and adjacent Saposa Island, which was the base for the barges of the 42nd Landing Craft Company. Lieutenant Masahiro Kurimato who served on Buka Island and Bonis Peninsula in 1945 reported that:

> 'A Japanese Observation Post was located on Mount Bei on Buka Island, which was 1312 feet high. Using high-powered binoculars from this vantage point, they could observe the activity of the Australians on Soraken and adjacent islands. Barges were observed making their way up the coast to Saposa Island. They then realised that a landing north of Soraken Plantation was a probability. They were also aided by observation platforms built on high trees along the coast.'[6]

Today, detritus from the battle more than half a century ago can still be seen on Porton beach in the rusted skeletons of two Allied landing barges. These stand sentinel on the

[6] Letter to John Feltham.

lonely reef in shallow water where they first grounded while under murderous Japanese fire. One of these wrecks has a tragic story to tell but it is also the keeper of other secrets which will never be known. The local natives from Chabai shun this barge as they sense its ghastly past. Old bomb craters made by the supporting Royal New Zealand Air Force Corsairs line the beach and are now filled with tangled debris, undergrowth, stagnant pools and bright green sludge.

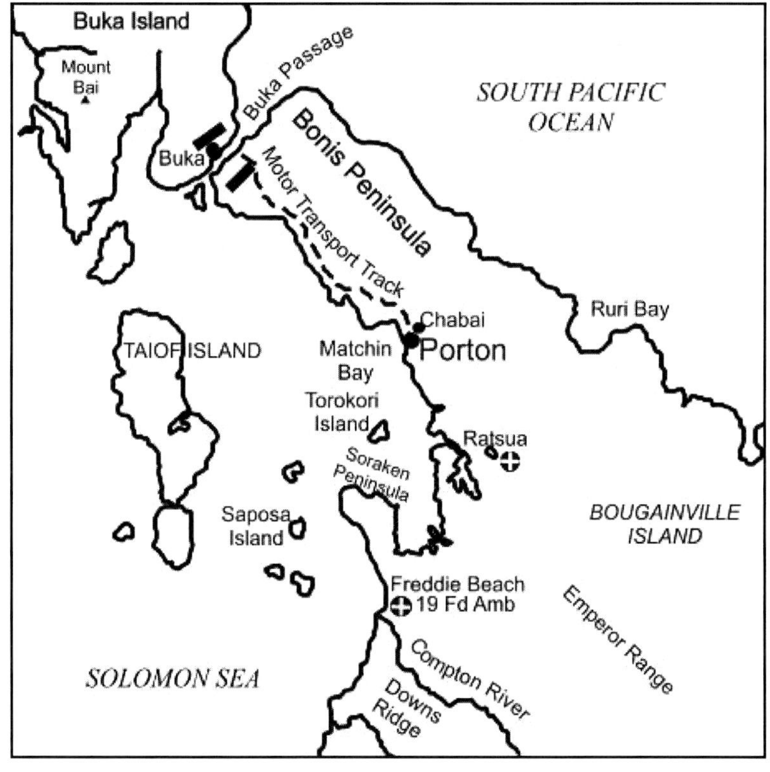

Bonis Peninsula

2 The Politicians

The full facts about this little-known episode in the Pacific War were not made public at the time of the action, nor since the war, apart from a few short articles in military magazines such as *Wartime* published by the Australian War Memorial. Historians paid scant attention to an operation which could have been seen as only a limited affray. The Porton battle rated a minor mention in the Australian press at the time and after that nothing more was heard of it. On June 11 1945 a short article appeared on page 3 of the Melbourne *Argus* headed 'New landing on North Bougainville: Australians meet opposition". Factual and brief, it mentions only that Australians came under fire at Porton Plantation.

All this changed in 2002 when Murray McCloskey, an enterprising journalist with Channel 7 television, made an informative documentary about the battle. Seen on Anzac Day that year, it was the first time most Australians had heard of Porton Plantation.

In 1945 there were several reasons for this lack of publicity. One was the fact that American General Douglas MacArthur, the Commander-in-Chief of the South West Pacific Area [S.W.P.A.], controlled all news communiqués concerning the progress of the war, and he made certain the news concentrated on the campaigns of the American troops and their victories. Australian participation in the conflict was rarely acknowledged by him.

> 'American reluctance to give due credit to the Australian role in the fighting was well established.

> Communiques describing Australian successes were issued attributing the victories to "Allied troops". If only American troops were involved, the GIs were given full credit.'[7]

During much of the Pacific war the Australian people were kept in ignorance of the extent of their Army's involvement and there was wide-spread public anger when the facts were revealed in the later stages of the war:

> 'Whereas in January [1945] the General Headquarters communiqué named all the American Divisions….and whence they had come,…the Australian formations and Commanders remained anonymous for weeks and, in most instances, months.'[8]

A second reason for the silence following Porton was that the Commander-in-Chief of the Australian Military Forces, General Sir Thomas Blamey, was currently attracting trenchant criticism in the Australian Press and Parliament for some of his strategies in the war in the Pacific:

> 'Rarely have the policies of any military commander been examined in such detail, and criticized to such an extent, while those policies were being carried out.'[9]

The *Sydney Morning Herald* in April 1945 challenged Blamey's decision to commit Australian servicemen to unnecessary fighting:

[7] *The Unnecessary War*, Peter Charlton, Macmillan Australia, 1983, p100

[8] *At War with the 31/51st Infantry Battalion (A.I.F.)* , Major W.E. Hughes MBE RL, Church Archivist Press, 1993, p124.

[9] *The Unnecessary War*, Peter Charlton, Macmillan Australia, 1983, p112

> 'If there are sound military or political reasons for exterminating the Japanese in the islands, under conditions of "war at its worst, and in the worst country imaginable", they should be stated'.[10]

During his distinguished and much-decorated Army career in WWI, Blamey had earned a reputation as a competent leader and military tactician. But in later years, as Commander of the Australian military forces in the Pacific during WWII, he was surrounded by controversy.

Some professional jealousy and antagonism, prompted by Blamey's past successes as well as his then position as head of the Army, was inevitable. However, his abrasive personality and ruthless treatment of subordinate commanders, e.g., Lieutenant General Rowell, Major General Allen, and Brigadier Potts who were relieved of their commands in New Guinea on General MacArthur's orders, won him many enemies in Parliament, among his commanders, and among his front-line troops.[11] In 1942 Blamey summarily cancelled the accreditation of the Australian Broadcasting Commission's star war correspondent, Chester Wilmot, when he criticized the Commander-in-Chief in New Guinea and questioned his competence.[12]

During the closing stages of the war the hostility Blamey was facing in Parliament was due largely to his controversial "mopping-up" campaigns in the islands. These were operations aimed at eliminating the scattered Japanese units that had become isolated and abandoned on the Pacific islands in 1943 after the war had moved on to the Phillipines. With their lines of communication cut,

[10] *Sydney Morning Herald*, 17 April 1945. Taken from *The Unnecessary War*, Peter Charlton, Macmillan Australia, 1993, p112.

[11] http://www.diggerhistory.info/pages-leaders/ww2/blamey.htm p7

[12] *Chester Wilmot Reports*, Neil McDonald, ABC Books, 2004

the enemy posed no further threat to Australian security. In time, without resupply, it was expected they would "wither on the vine".

The offensives were very contentious. They were responsible for the ongoing and unnecessary loss of many Australian lives in places which had clearly been by-passed by the war. It was obvious in 1945 that the Commander-in-Chief didn't need the added damaging publicity of Porton's deadly fiasco.

Blamey's detractors regarded him as a political opportunist. These "final campaigns" were perceived to have,

> 'Little impact on the eventual course of the war, [they were] campaigns that had more to do with personal ambition and political dreaming than with the demands of considered, careful, productive strategy.'[13]

Attention was also being drawn to the fact that

> 'For the first time an Australian General led an Australian Army in operations in pursuit of Australian political objectives".[14]

The fighting men believed this to be a "politicians' war." Peter Charlton in his book *The Unnecessary War* maintains it was:

> 'A general's war. The war of Sir Thomas Blamey. It was his decisions that launched the offensives in New Guinea and Bougainville. The politicians simply went along – or were taken – for the ride'.[15]

[13] *The Unnecessary War,* Peter Charlton, Macmillan Australia, 1983, 30

[14] http://www.diggerhistory.info/pages-leaders/ww2/blamey.htm p8

[15] *The Unnecessary War*, Peter Charlton, Macmillan Australia, 1983, p 2.

General Thomas Blamey in safari style uniform insepecting troops.

Blamey later became the first Field Marshall in Australian history. In his biography, *Blamey. The Commander–in-Chief,* David Horner writes:

> 'The operations of the First Australian Army in the New Guinea area and the 1st Australian Corps in Borneo between March and the end of July 1945 are some of the most contentious in Australian military history.' [16]

It was obvious therefore, in June 1945, that the Porton battle with its 56 per cent casualty rate would have made shocking news headlines.

Powerful leaders' political ambitions were not the only reasons for the years of silence after the Porton battle. The

[16] *Blamey. The Commander-in-Chief,* David Horner, Allen & Unwin, 1998, p510

testimonies of the battle survivors have shown that, from the beginning, serious doubts about the quality of the battle planning were expressed by the company commanders involved. The operation was considered by those officers to be too risky. Although the strategy as planned had succeeded on previous occasions, at Toko in the south and at Soraken, they were convinced that at Porton there would be too few men and too few resources available for this task. The commanders advised that it should not go ahead.

In addition to the faulty organization, and with no reason given, Brigade was requiring the commanders to implement the plan hastily, thus allowing little time for adequate preparation. The company commanders' reports show that they were critical of the decision to make the assault under these conditions. Their objections were overruled. The battle went ahead, with a predictable outcome, so nothing more was heard of it.

As there was no publicity, the small Australian assault force which fought so courageously on that beach received no recognition for the major part it played in the action. It was not revealed that for more than three days and nights on Porton beach those 190 men came face-to-face with a desperate enemy who proved to be not only fanatically determined but also vastly superior in arms and numbers. There was at all times a very real possibility that the assault force could be overwhelmed and annihilated by the sheer numbers of the Japanese defenders. The survivors endured unimaginable horror and privation before their final rescue was achieved on the morning of the fourth day.

The troops had also quickly discovered that the Japanese Imperial Naval Force was not the only deadly enemy waiting for them at Porton. Beneath the sparkling waters of the bay lurked the sharp coral reef which was to take an enormous toll of their manpower, weapons and supplies. The tropical heat, disease, dehydration and exposure, and the foetid swamps also claimed victims. Jungle wilderness pressed in on every landward side and the Australians were cruelly reminded that the rampant vegetation not only concealed the enemy – it caused good men to become utterly disoriented. And it killed them.

Photo taken from a Boomerang plane shows the wrecked jetties and stranded barges

The War 3

Following the outbreak of the Pacific war in December 1941 Japanese forces moved south from Japan, China and Malaya with alarming speed to attack and occupy other areas in the south-west Pacific basin. After Singapore fell in February 1942 it was realized by Australians that some of these territories, such as New Guinea, Timor, and the Solomon Islands, were almost on their doorstep.

Rabaul, also captured by the Japanese in 1942, provided them with an important strategic naval and airforce base for the imminent conquest of the Solomons. The Japanese went on to occupy Buka and Bougainville in 1942 and constructed airstrips on both islands. Their intention in taking over the Solomon Islands chain was to cut Australia's line of communication with the United States. In New Guinea however their rapid advance was halted in late 1942 by Australian forces at Milne Bay and Kokoda.

The American Marines then took on the task of expelling the Japanese troops who had occupied the Solomons. They achieved this by February 1943 after some bitter and costly battles on Tulagi and Guadalcanal islands. The Japanese drive south had also been checked in 1942 at the battles of the Coral Sea and Midway, giving the Americans, with their superior aircraft carriers, control of the seas in the area.

In November 1943 the Americans established a base at Torokina on Bougainville in order to set up their airfields and port facilities. This cut the Japanese lines of communication in the Solomon Islands and their bases on Bougainville and Buka Islands were neutralised.

From that time the Japanese army on these islands received no more reinforcements, ammunition, medical or food supplies. They were isolated with no hope of rescue, fell prey to disease, and had to cultivate vegetable gardens in order to feed their troops. Peter Charlton wrote in *The Unnecessary War:*

> 'During the latter half of 1944, approximately 35 per cent of the Japanese force were on gardening and fishing duty, 15 per cent were on transport duty, 30 per cent were sick, and 20 per cent [were] in the forward areas.'[17]

At Torokina the Americans fortified themselves behind a shallow perimeter and, with control of the air and the sea, they made no move to engage the Japanese; "a policy of live-and-let-live [was] pursued by both sides." However, enemy numbers had been seriously underestimated by the Allies. Instead of an army of about 17,000 men, as they thought, it was later shown that there were still 30,000 – 40,000 Japanese soldiers and marines occupying much of Bougainville at that time, in garrisons, gardens, and small pockets of resistance. They remained a well-organised though diminishing force but, without access to supplies, they were reluctant to fight. These enemy troops were satisfied to maintain an unofficial truce with the Americans.[18]

When General Douglas Macarthur moved the American forces north from the New Guinea area in December 1944 to recapture the Phillipines in his push towards Tokyo, the Australian 2nd Corps headed by Lieutenant General Stan Savige, took over the base at Torokina. Savige, 51 years

[17] *The Unnecessary War*, Peter Charlton, Macmillan Australia, 1983, p37

[18] Ibid. p37.

old, was an old comrade and friend of Blamey's from WWI.

The Australians were to have a garrison role in Bougainville with five Brigades, all militia formations. Of the twelve battalions involved, eight came from Queensland. Macarthur's instructions to General Blamey were:

> 'Australian forces [should] assume responsibility for the continued neutralization of the Japanese in Australian and British Territories and Mandates in the South-West Pacific area.'

He also stated:

> 'The enemy garrisons that have been by-passed in New Guinea and the Solomons represent no menace to current or future operations. Their capacity for organized offensive effort has passed. The various processes of attrition will eventually account for their disposition. The actual time of their destruction is of little or no importance and their influence as a contributing fact to the war is already negligible. The actual process of their immediate destruction by assault methods would unquestionably involve heavy loss of life without adequate compensating strategic advantages.'[20]

While it seemed apparent that the Japanese, if left alone, would eventually perish from disease and starvation, General Blamey nevertheless - ambiguously - stated his intention, "By offensive action to destroy enemy resistance without committing major forces". At the same time he

[20] *At War with the 31/51st Infantry Battalion*, Major W.E. Hughes MBE RL, Church Archivist Press, 1993, p184

issued instructions to his commanders, "You should seek out the Japs and destroy them."

Accordingly, only three days after Lieutenant General Savige took over from the Americans at Torokina the Australians began their offensive action. A platoon attacked and captured a small Japanese outpost at Little George Hill, a small knoll close to Torokina and only 50 yards from the American lines. This was the troops' first action in Bougainville apart from patrolling and for the enemy it marked the end of the unofficial truce.[21]

Many Australian servicemen were to lose their lives in the much disputed "mopping-up" campaigns which followed in the final days of the Pacific War. Peter Charlton explains why the troops at that time were chronically hampered by lack of tactical resources:

> 'Because MacArthur did not think these campaigns were worth fighting, and because his headquarters virtually controlled the equipment of war in the area, these campaigns were fought with insufficient shipping, artillery, tanks, medical supplies even – all the necessities of a modern war.'[22]

The battles were achieving nothing for Australian defence or the course of the war. They were widely criticized for being not only unnecessary but also a costly waste of manpower and materials - and the men doing the fighting knew it. During the nine months of combat in Bougainville alone, 516 Australian servicemen were killed or died of wounds and 1,572 were badly wounded - more than in the

[21] *The Unnecessary War*, Peter Charlton, Macmillan Australia, 1983, pp40, 41.

[22] Ibid. p1.

ten years of the Vietnam War.[23]

In *The Unnecessary War* Peter Charlton quotes the critical comments of some of the Bougainville commanders at that time. Lieutenant Colonel Byrne, Commanding Officer of 42nd Battalion, had no illusions about the role of his troops:

> 'I think that collectively the officers and men did a grand job. It was a filthy country; they were fighting what appeared to be a useless campaign and they knew it. Men are not fools and even though each man realised he was fighting for something which could benefit his country very little [and in addition his fighting received very little credit or publicity] he carried out orders energetically and in a very fine spirit'.[24]

Major N.I. Winning, a former 9th Division Company Commander who, with his 2/8th Commando Squadron had spent nearly a month assessing the overall situation in Bougainville, came to this conclusion:

> 'It's nothing but a bloody self-supporting prisoner-of-war camp. To fight a war here and provoke hostilities will be nothing more than sinful destruction and wastage of bloody fine men who deserve to be laid off and sent home to their people.'[25]

Among these fine fighting men were the troops who formed the five militia (CMF) brigades of Lieutenant General Savige's occupying 2nd Corps. However, they

[23] *The Unnecessary War*, Peter Charlton, Macmillan Australia, 1983, p60.

[24] Ibid. p62

[25] Ibid. p33

were not the raw inexperienced "chocos" who were often disdainfully referred to by the AIF in the early part of the war as "chocolate soldiers" - those who would melt if the heat was turned up or they were exposed to the sun. With the exception of the 23rd Brigade, they had all seen active service in New Guinea and many were seasoned jungle fighters.

Backed by his own considerable experience, ex-Porton battle Platoon Commander Lieutenant F. (Blue) Reiter, M.C., M.M., M.I.D. holds very firm views about the role played by the CMF in wartime:

> 'The men of the CMF, often called "chocos", were as good as any AIF and I was proud to have served with them. I should know as I had three years AIF and three years CMF. There should have been only one AMF [Australian Military Force]. The press has a lot to answer for as they gave better coverage to the AIF. It was the "chocos" that first took on the Japs on the Kokoda Track and Milne Bay'.

The Battalions 4

The 31st/51st Battalion which was heavily involved in the Porton battle was a combined North Queensland militia unit which later formed part of the 11th Brigade. The 31st Battalion was Townsville-based and in early 1942 had been allocated the defence of the Townsville area; at the same time the 51st Battalion from Cairns and the Atherton Tableland was given the responsibility for the defence of the Cairns area. Both battalions had been depleted in numbers after the government demobilized many servicemen to meet the call for extra manpower in essential industries. Major W. Hughes records:

> 'In February 1943 the 31st and 51st Infantry Battalions suffered considerably when rural workers were discharged. In April [they] were brought up to full strength by amalgamating both units and the new unit was named the 31st/51st Infantry Battalion.'[26]

After July 1943 the Battalion as part of 11th Brigade spent more than twelve months in Merauke, Dutch New Guinea, where their mission was to protect the air base and several outposts. Merauke was under intermittent air attack by the Japanese during 1943. The 31st/51st Battalion carried out long-range patrolling operations in this tropical,

[26] *At War with the 31/51st Infantry Battalion*, Major W.E. Hughes MBE RL, Church Archivist Press, 1993, p58

disease-ridden, swampy terrain, traversing many kilometres of sluggish waterways in small craft and engaging heavily with the enemy on several occasions.[27]

Many derogatory observations were made about Dutch New Guinea by the servicemen who were there in WWII. Lieutenant Blue Reiter was in Merauke with the 11th Brigade and his opinion was shared by his mates:

> 'Merauke was the arsehole of the world…it was the worst place I have ever seen in the whole of the war – just the swamps and the stink and the stench of everything! We were doing a lot of patrolling because they never knew if the Japs were going to come over the mountains or down along the coast.'

The 31st/51st Infantry Battalion was gazetted an AIF Battalion in July 1944 and was withdrawn from Merauke in August 1944 – to the huge relief of all concerned.

After four months in Australia, the Battalion departed Brisbane aboard a Victory Class ship *Sea Snipe* bound for Bougainville and arrived at Torokina on December 10. In keeping with General Blamey's instructions, Lieutenant General Savige at 2nd Corps Headquarters had formulated a three-phase strategic plan to attack and destroy the Japanese in the north, east and south of the island simultaneously. The 11th Brigade was allotted the task of pushing northward to force the enemy into the narrow Bonis Peninsula and there destroying them. Accordingly, the 31st/51st Battalion and the 26th Battalion, both 11th Brigade units, spent the

[27] *At War with the 31/51st Infantry Battalion,* Major W.E. Hughes MBE RL, Church Archivist Press, 1993, pp104,105.

following six weeks fighting their way up the west coast to achieve this result.

For the troops of the 31st/51st Battalion this was their first major campaign. Apart from occasional patrol and outpost skirmishes they had not previously been in action as a Battalion. However, during the drive northward they had successfully engaged the Japanese at the battles of Tsimba Ridge, the Genga and Gillman Rivers, Downs Ridge and also on the Numa Numa Trail. The unit suffered heavy casualties with 39 killed and 90 wounded, but despite this violent beginning it had proved itself a very competent fighting force.

> 'A Japanese Officer stated afterwards that he did not think it possible that the Australians could have received so much punishment and still have persisted in their attacks.'[28]

In February 1945 the battalion was relieved at Downs Ridge by the 26th Battalion which continued the determined advance northwards and by June 1945 they had reached Ratsua on the Bonis Peninsula. An 11th Brigade diarist wrote that the campaign had been one of:

> 'Holding a superior number of enemy by the aggressive action of a tired depleted Battalion – Companies were no more than half strength and had been in the forward areas continuously for four months.'

The 26th Battalion's fighting strength on June 3 was only 23 officers and 353 other ranks.

[28] *At War with the 31/51st Infantry Battalion*, Major W.E. Hughes MBE RL, Church Archivist Press, 1993, p178.

The 31st/51st Battalion, having had a period of rest, reorganization and training at Torokina, then joined them at Ratsua. The Australians had discovered that the Japanese on Bougainville continued to maintain strong defensive positions in their scattered garrisons and native gardens. They resisted stubbornly and always hit back hard.

The Battle Plan 5

By June 1945 the 11th Brigade had been instrumental in pushing the enemy back into a decreasing area on the Bonis Peninsula. Brigade now proposed that having reached Ratsua, the 26th Battalion and the 31st/51st Battalion should secure a line across the narrow neck of the peninsula from Porton Plantation on the west coast to Ruri Bay on the east, a distance of approximately 6 kilometres. The 26th Battalion and part of the 31st/51st Battalion were to operate on the east side of the peninsula and eventually join up with the remainder of the 31st/51st Battalion on the west. It was intended that the enemy should be contained north of this line.[29]

As part of this plan, and as soon as resistance had been broken in the Ratsua area, a small sea-borne force was to make a pre-dawn landing behind the Japanese lines at Porton Beach, about 8 kilometres north of the Soraken Peninsula. The purpose of this outflanking move, to take place on June 8, was intended to:

> '(1) Bring pressure to bear behind the forward enemy position to cause a withdrawal.
>
> (2) Establish a beachhead through which supplies could be sent by barge for further operations northwards.'[30]

Details of the projected operation appear in the Battalion's Intelligence Report which covers the pre-battle

[29] *At War with the 31/51st Infantry Battalion*, Major W.E. Hughes MBE RL, Church Archivist Press, 1993, p208.

[30] 31/51 Australian Infantry Battalion (AIF) Confidential Report written 9 July, 1945, p27

conference held on June 5 at Ratsua. The conference was presided over by Lieutenant Colonel J.L.A. Kelly D.S.O. [C.O. 31st/51st Australian Infantry Battalion]. Also present were Major R.G. [Dick] Sampson M.C. [Battle 2 I/C], Captain H.C. [Clyde] Downs M.I.D. [O.C. "A" Company], and Captain A.L. [Blue] Shilton M.C. [O.C. "C" Company]. The Section and Detachment commanders also attended.

The report gave the outline of the plan and also the factors which had been discussed, such as the landing craft suitable for the landing; the time, place and method of landing; the degree of penetration; the ammunition and supplies necessary for the operation, and intercommunication.[31]

On June 6 orders were received that the Porton operation would take place on the night June 7/8. It was intended that a combined assault force of approximately 190 men would be involved, led by Captain Clyde Downs with Captain Blue Shilton as 2 I/C and beachmaster. The force would be comprised of all of "A" Company and a Platoon of "C" Company, supported by detachments of engineers, artillery, signals, field ambulance and Australian Army Service Corps. [AASC] A flame-throwers platoon and one other platoon from "C" Company were to reinforce the beachhead on the night of June 8/9.[32]

The C.O. of the assault, Captain Clyde Downs M.I.D., was married, with two children, and prior to WWII was a chartered accountant and a company manager and secretary on the Atherton Tableland. Like his father, Matthew Downs, who served for 15 months in the Boer War with the 1st Imperial N.S.W. Rifles, Clyde Downs was a proficient rifleman and had been a member of the 51st Battalion since

[31] 31/51 Australian Infantry Battalion (AIF) Confidential Report written 9 July, 1945, p27.

[32] Ibid. p28.

1936. He remained O.C. "A" Company $31^{st}/51^{st}$ from 1943 until his death in action in 1945.

At 38 years of age Downs was considerably older than his troops, many of whom were 18 or 19 year-old "Curtin conscripts". It was reported that he looked on them as "family" and several spoke of him as being like a father to them. They called him "the Skipper". He gained M.I.D. distinction at the Battle of Tsimba Ridge and his name was given to Downs Ridge after that successful engagement. In a letter to his brother Amos in the closing days of the war, he wrote:

> 'Well the war seems to be advancing pretty rapidly these days. Wouldn't be surprised if it is all over by Xmas. Hope so anyway. They can call it off as soon as they like as far as I am concerned. I'll be 39 next month. Still I think I will manage to see it through now that it has gone this far.
>
> 'This Bougainville show seems to get plenty of publicity in the press. Suppose you saw where I managed to peg out the family name here. However I don't think I will want to claim it after the war.
>
> 'Still have some of the old crowd with me. They are a good crowd.'

The O.C. "C" Company, Captain A.L. [Blue] Shilton M.C., was a 27 year-old accountant from Melbourne. He was married, and a three-week-old infant daughter was his only child. Following his family tradition of military service, Shilton joined the Victorian Scottish Regiment as a cadet in 1935, enlisted in 2/5 Battalion AIF in 1939 and was commissioned in 1940. After serving 2 years in the Western Desert, Syria and Palestine, he joined the 31st Battalion in early 1943, was soon promoted to Captain and was O.C.

AWM093132. Captain Stuart Leslie 2nd from right (sitting) O.C. 42nd Landing Craft Coy with Ravi, the head Native Pilot and crew members. This was the only ALCA to get off the beach without being stranded in the evacuation. The 42nd. suffered heavy casualties.

"C" Company 31st/51st from June 1943 to October 1945.

Captain Shilton was a hard task-master ("Simon Legree"!) but his men held him in the highest esteem. In battle he would not ask his troops to do anything that he would not do himself. Shilton was awarded an M.C. for bravery at the battle of the Genga River three months prior to Porton, and he was to suffer wounds at Porton.[33]

The battle 2 I/C at Porton, Major Dick Sampson M.C., also had a strong military tradition. He was the son of Boer War and WWI veteran Colonel Burford Sampson D.S.O. who later became a politician and had for a time been the C.O. 51st Battalion. Dick progressed from the militia to the AIF 6th Division in 1939. He served as a lieutenant in the Middle East, Greece and Crete, and won his M.C. in Greece.

The barges which were necessary for the Porton landing were to be provided by the 42nd Landing Craft Company Royal Australian Engineers [R.A.E.] led by Captain Stuart Leslie. Many of this Company, including Leslie, had served in Papua New Guinea with 2/8th Armoured Regiment. After this unit was disbanded in 1943 they were seconded in 1944 into the 42nd Australian Landing Craft Company where they received intense training at the base at Toorbul Point in Queensland.

There had been an acute shortage of water transport and serviceable landing barges in Bougainville for some time and those at hand were being used in many areas along the coast for supply as well as for movement of personnel. Nevertheless, Captain Leslie was able to make three LC [Landing Craft]15s and three ALCAs [Armoured Landing

[33] *Lives and Times*, ed. John Gardner.

Craft Assault] available to this operation.

The origin of the ALCA is described by Major W. Hughes in his book which details the history of the 31st/51st Infantry Battalion:

> 'They were donated to the 13 Small Ships' Company on Puriata Island just off the shore from Torokina, by the British Navy when the aircraft carrier H.M.S. Glory visited Empress Augusta Bay. These armour-plated vessels had been used in the invasion of Normandy. Their laminated plywood bottoms were subject to attacks by tropical marine borers which was probably why the barge holed on the reef at Porton.'[34]

Although armoured, the barges provided little protection for the gunners who manned the Browning and Vickers machine-guns.

Sapper Allan Graham, a Browning gunner in the 42nd Landing Craft Company at Porton, affectionately described his association with the *Yorkshire Rose:*

> 'ALCAs were small landing craft armed with .5 Browning machine guns forward and twin Vickers aft. *Yorkshire Rose* [my craft] was named by the Royal Marine Commandos and had the scroll in white on the tiny engine-room door along with places it had been, in gold paint – North Africa, Sicily and Salerno. The *Rose* never let us down and I do not think we let the Commandos down. The [painted] engine-room door is now believed to be in the Australian War Museum'.

[34] *At War with the 31/51st Infantry Battalion*, Major W.E.Hughes MBE RL, Church Archivist Press, 1993, p250

The pre-battle conference at Ratsua had determined that the landing at Porton beach was to be made in two waves, each consisting of three barges. The first wave would be comprised of the three armoured ALCAs which were to carry personnel from both Company Headquarters and "A" Company, including the C.O. Captain Clyde Downs. The second wave was to be made up of three bigger and heavier barges, Australian-made LCl5s, which would hold the engineer stores, supplies, ammunition, close support weapons and remaining personnel under the command of 2 I/C and beachmaster Captain Shilton. The beachmaster's role was to coordinate the movement of troops and supplies on the beach.[35]

[35] 31/51st Infantry Battalion (AIF) Confidential Report

Battle Plan Doubts 6

Following the battle conference, reports by the company commanders showed concern about what they perceived to be serious faults in the planning. The project appeared to have been put together too hastily. They thought there had been no recognition by the planners that, with insufficient men and support troops, a shortage of serviceable landing craft and deficiencies in ammunition and supplies, this assault had little hope of success. The perception was later borne out in the accounts of the troops who had fought and survived, under these incredible handicaps.

There was a firmly-held belief amongst the men, which still holds currency to-day, that the "Porton show" was hurriedly brought forward for the benefit of General Blamey who was expected to be in the area at that time. Major W.E. Hughes in his history of the 31/51^{s} Infantry Battalion wrote of the Commander-in-Chief's intended visit:

> 'Just after the 31st/51st Battalion arrived on Soraken Peninsula General Blamey decided on a visit. He and his entourage which included Lieutenant General Savige, C.O. of the 2nd Australian Corps, Torokina, landed by sea and were located on Saposa Island. When word was received of the intended visit, Lieutenant Arthur Graham, O.C. 2 Platoon 16 Field Company (R.A.E.), organized a Platoon of his engineers to work for about two weeks preparing suitable accommodation for him and his staff. One of the luxuries bestowed upon him was the installation of a power generator.

'He was allotted a special protection group armed with Owen guns, and a group of expert rifle-men provided him with an escort whenever he visited Brigade and Battalion Headquarters. During the Porton Plantation battle General Blamey and his entourage were on Saposa Island within distant view of the conflict area. At one stage of the battle when returning from a fishing trip, his launch picked up a soldier who had swum from Porton.'[36]

Captain A.L. (Blue) Shilton M.C., O.C "C" Coy. 31st/51st Inf Bn. Beachmaster at Porton, June 1945, Bougainville.

Because of the pre-battle TacR (tactical reconnaissance) reports of a significant build-up of enemy strength in the

[36] *At War with the 31/5st Infantry Battalion*, Major W.E. Hughes MBE RL Church Archivist Press, 1993, p206

Porton area, Brigade Commander J.R. Stevenson had requested a softening up aerial attack on the target before the landing, but 2nd Corps at base in Torokina did not consider it a suitable target.[37] Captain Downs also asked for air cover at the time of the landing. This was refused. At the planning stage of this battle the frustration felt by the officers at every level of command is seen in Captain Blue Shilton's report. Backed by his own past experience and knowledge of field-craft he was very critical of the Porton plan:

> 'Clyde Downs, Dick Sampson and I objected to the small number of troops [and] no plan of withdrawal or reinforcement except by 15 Platoon "C" Company on the night following the landing. No notice was taken of these objections and [they] were dismissed out of hand.
>
> 'The plan was for "A"Company to advance into the "never never" [following the landing]. No explanation of the "never never" was given. Apparently no overland reconnaissance had been made of the area between Ratsua and Porton and no mention made of it.
>
> 'From my point of view, and I'm sure that of all those present who were to participate, it was a very sketchy and risky plan with no real perception of what could go wrong. So much for forward planning, or lack of it.'

A report was also made by Major Dick Sampson M.C. He endorsed Captain Shilton's concerns. Having had

[37] *Australia in the War of 1939-1945. Volume V11 The Final Campaigns*, Gavin Long,

front-line experience in other theatres of war, he knew the essential requirements for a successful amphibious landing such as that planned at Porton. In careful detail he drew attention to the need for proper identification of landing points, accurate intelligence regarding enemy strength, and the absolute imperative of having sufficient men and ammunition supplies to do the job, as well as to provide for all possible eventualities.

Major Dick Sampson, M.C.

'I visited Captains Downs and Shilton on the afternoon of June 7 on behalf of the Commanding Officer [Brigadier Stevenson] to see that final arrangements were completed. Captain Downs was completing the draft of his Operation Order. Both he and Captain Shilton were not satisfied with the strength of the force and the question of reserves if strong opposition was met with. The Brigade C.O. said that if necessary another Company from Battalion Headquarters would be sent.'

Serious doubts about the coming operation were also being expressed by Captain Stuart Leslie, O.C. of the 42nd Landing Craft Company. He was concerned about having to bring his unserviceable barges in to the beach through a reef which had been shown in the pre-battle aerial survey reports to be dangerous:

> 'Prior to the operation we were shown aerial reconnaissance photos of the Porton area and it was obvious there were many reefs close in to shore. As set out in the official report most of the ALCAs

were unserviceable but were speedily patched up. The jetties were [also] unserviceable and it would be very difficult to land the troops on the shore except at high tide.

> 'I pointed out to Brigadier Stevenson the impossibility of achieving a successful landing here because of the reefs and our unseaworthy landing craft and the wrecked jetties. Notwithstanding this, we were required to land a Company group of 31st/51st Aust Infantry Battalion early in the morning of June 8 1945.'

Lieutenant Arthur Graham M.C., OC of 2 Platoon 16 Field Company [R.A.E.], having returned to Ratsua on June 7 after a brief visit to Torokina, was surprised to find Corporal Ben Bertram and his Section of 2 Platoon all kitted out in battle gear. He reported:

> 'It was then I learned a landing at Porton Plantation was intended. Since Ben had no watch nor compass, I passed mine on loan to him and wished them good fortune. Perhaps I was not the only one confused and ill-informed.'

There was a general feeling of apprehension and lack of preparedness amongst the troops prior to the proposed landing and this was evident in their recollections of that time. No-one seemed to know what to expect.

One 8 Platoon veteran had reason to remember the day before the Porton landing:

> 'I first heard of Porton the day before we landed there. 8 Platoon "A" Company was called together and it was explained what was to happen early next morning. Lieutenant Bill Evans, Platoon

Commander, showed sketch maps and gave details. We were told we would be loaded aboard a landing craft at 2 o'clock next morning. One man refused to go claiming, "It would be suicide". He was advised by officers and N.C.O.s but steadfastly refused to go. I read recently that he died in New Zealand.'

Lieutenant Blue Reiter M.C., M.M., M.I.D., 9 Platoon Commander, A" Coy. 31st/51st Bn A.I.F Bougainville June 1945.

Lieutenant Blue Reiter knew about the Porton plan. He was the commander of 9 Platoon "A" Company and a five-times-wounded veteran of the Middle East, Greece, Crete, Egypt and New Guinea campaigns, who had been a farmer in Victoria prior to WW II. Blue enlisted in the 2/5Battalion on the first day of WW II and after active service in the Middle East and Greece he was taken prisoner in Crete. He escaped and fought with partisans for six months until he and some other troops were able to steal a fishing boat, hoist a German flag, and head out into the Mediterranean. They were picked up by a British submarine and returned to their unit.

Showing himself in conflict to be fearless, wise and battle-wise, Blue also proved himself a champion of justice and the under-dog. His first concern was always the welfare of his men, and his cheerful disdain of authority did not diminish the respect and esteem shown him by the men who fought alongside him, regardless of their rank.

Blue knew about Porton because two weeks previously he had been given compassionate leave to attend his father's funeral in Melbourne. Brigade instructed him to return to Soraken by June 6; he was told in confidence that the assault was to take place at Porton on June 8. He expressed the current cynical view:

> 'I often wondered if the show was put on as General Blamey was to be in the area'.

Private Len [Stiffy] Flynn seemed to be as confused by events pre-Porton as his mates:

> 'The night of June 7 was like any other night except for the fact that we were mulling over where we would be on the 8th – especially when we were informed we were to do an amphibious landing on that day at a place called Porton. Porton? Where was it? Never heard of it before. We were then told it was in enemy territory beyond our front line. Bodies rested that night but minds didn't and we wondered what lay ahead.'

As darkness gathered on the night of June 7 the Battalion's proposed landing was imminent. The plans had been made, but it was clear that the men had not been made ready; their reports show that they were acutely aware of the fact. However, the stage was now set for the drama of the Battle of Porton Plantation.

As it unfolded, this drama was to resemble classical Greek tragedy which progresses relentlessly through the grim acts to reach a disastrous conclusion - a pre-ordained conclusion which is made inevitable from the beginning. However, unlike Greek tragedy in which there is no escape from the ultimate catastrophe, for the fighting men of Porton in the darkest hours of their ordeal there was always hope and courage and the best of mates alongside.

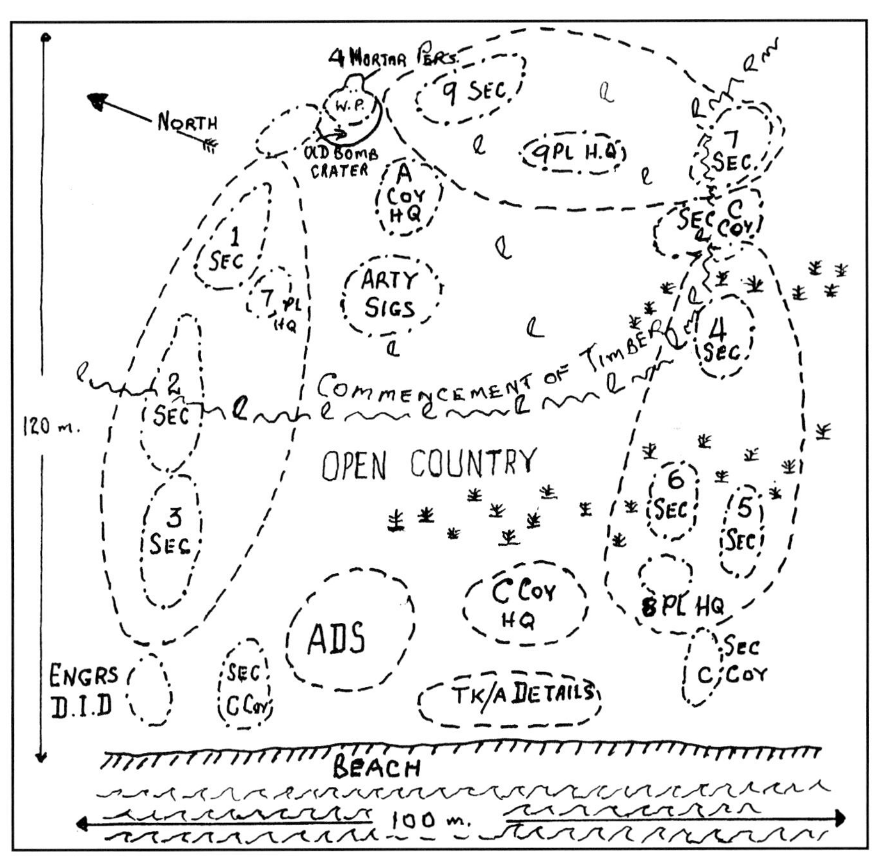

Diagramatic sketch A Coy Perimeter 8 June, Porton
Not drawn to scale.

The Landing 7

As the barges approached Porton beach at 3.45 a.m. on the day of the landing the world was profoundly dark. There was no moon and no hint yet of the sunrise which would usher in a momentous day.

> 'It was a calm night and the craft moved at about three-quarter speed to within 1000 metres of the assault beach by 3.45 a.m. The ALCAs moved in and about fifteen minutes later the LC15s were signalled in. Moving at quarter speed we got to within about 100 metres of the shore when the barges beached, the ramp was lowered and the troops waded ashore…..'

This was how Lieutenant Keith Scoble O.C. of the A.A.S.C. [Australian Army Service Corps] recalled the landing. He was in one of the LC15s and wrote the report at this time.

The pre-dawn landing on Porton beach on June 8 1945 was the first amphibious operation in the history of the 31st/51st Battalion,[38] and for the 42nd Landing Craft Company it was 'the most daunting task of the unit's war-time exploits.'[39] It was implemented by the 31st/51st Battalion which drew upon the elementary amphibious training given the troops at Yorkey's Knob and Ellis Beach near Cairns,

[38] War Diary of 31/51st Aust Infantry Battalion, p1

[39] *Sailors in Slouch Hats* ,ed. W. Rice, Dept. of Defence, 1999, p4

eighteen months before their embarkation for Bougainville. The landing was undertaken on the strength of three brief rehearsals at "Freddie" Beach near the Soraken Peninsula two days before the operation. It was later discovered that the Japs had been able to watch the rehearsals from their lookout on Buka Island.

After leaving "Freddie" Beach the first wave of three ALCAs reached Porton at 4.05 a.m according to plan. However, in the darkness the native pilot had taken them in 100 metres north of the planned landing site and, as Captain Leslie had feared, all the barges grounded on the coral reef. The pilot had missed the narrow channel leading through the reef to the jetty. This had been clearly marked in the pre-battle aerial photographs of the area and was known to Brigade.

Landing Craft Base on Saposa island

Captain Leslie noted in his report :

'On Saposa Is. we had a detachment of native pilots, the boss boy being Ravi who was quite intelligent. As most of our operations were conducted at night, particularly to the forward infantry base at Ratsua, it was necessary to take

> a pilot wherever we went so he could guide the craft through the reefs and other water hazards. We were completely in their hands and he could easily have led us into the Japanese anchorages or beaches.'

Major Dick Sampson's report had been explicit:

> 'Pre-war inhabitants of Porton who were available should have been closely examined regarding the suitability of the landing area'.

The pilot's error proved tragically costly in men and supplies and the official records demonstrate how his blunder affected the ultimate outcome of the battle.

At the beach, in darkness, the disembarking troops had to wade ashore from the grounded barges. They made their way for 50 metres over the reef and through waist-high water holding their packs and weapons aloft. Corporal J. [Ned] Marsterson of the Mortar Platoon recalled his painful introduction to Porton beach:

> 'When they dropped the front of the barge down we were some way out in the sea still in about one metre of water. When I jumped in I fell over and the fellow behind me jumped on my knee. I crawled ashore – I thought he'd broken my knee or put it out of joint.'[40]

Nevertheless, the first wave of men achieved total surprise and was able to land unopposed, penetrate the plantation verge and, still in darkness, dig in to establish a perimeter

[40] T.V. Documentary *The Savage Shore*, Murray McCloskey, 2002

about 150 metres inland. The 7th, 8th and 9th Platoons took up their allotted positions around the perimeter. The empty barges floated off the reef and returned to base at Saposa.[41]

The second wave of landing craft arrived at Porton at 4.35 a.m. There were two large LC15 stores barges which held engineer stores, supplies, ammunition and close support weapons; the third LC15 carried Captain Shilton and the men of 14 Platoon "C" Company with their Platoon leader Lieutenant Norm Gillman, together with a quantity of stores. Captain Shilton reported:

> '"A" Company got ashore in the 1st wave without a shot being fired. The barges used were the ALCAs, quiet-running ones, low silhouette and perfect for the job. The second wave consisted of three LC15s, large, noisy things which woke the dead when the ramps thumped down.'

Upon reaching Porton this second wave of landing craft also became grounded on the reef, 75 metres offshore. The men disembarked quickly from the leading barge and, carrying their weapons and packs made their way through the water to the beach as the previous troops had done. Their barge then refloated and returned to base.

One of the other two grounded LC15s was hard aground with the engine revving desperately as the coxswain tried to back it off the reef. Captain Shilton believes that the second stores barge, which was also carrying ammunition, mortars, A/tank gun, etc., was able to turn back after it first hit the reef. However, there appear to be no further reports on the fate of this LC15.

[41] 31/51st Aust Infantry Battalion (AIF) Confidential Report, p29

The noise of the second landing alerted the enemy. From their gun positions around the beach they opened up savagely with heavy and sustained automatic fire against the stranded stores barge and the disembarking men on the beach. This made it impossible for the troops to unload the heavy weapons and reserve ammunition and supplies.[42]It was decided that any salvaging of stores would have to be postponed until nightfall.

In the documentary *The Savage Shore*, Captain Shilton spoke of the men's surprise at the scale of enemy resistence:

> 'We got ashore and then the fun started because we had landed in the middle of quite a big Jap area. We were told there were not many Japs there!"

Intelligence reports had estimated that there were approximately 100 Japanese at Porton.

The grounded stores barge rapidly became the focus of enemy attention and any movement around the craft drew salvos of fire from automatic weapons.

As soon as Australian reconnaissance patrolling around the perimeter commenced it became apparent that the assault force had entered a deadly trap on Porton beach. The patrols quickly discovered that the perimeter was within an arc of enemy trenches and pill-boxes with a radius of about 400 metres. It was impossible for troops to advance inland because of these defences and it was equally impossible to retreat because of the reef and continuous Japanese gunfire. Bracketing fire was now coming in behind the landed troops from positions on both the left and right flanks:

[42] 31/51st Aust Infantry Battalion (AIF) Confidential Report, p29.

> 'A 9 Platoon patrol led by Sergeant Garth Tickle moved east ... and engaged an enemy patrol. In this engagement the enemy fired on the Platoon perimeter in the rear of the patrol, and large parties of the enemy were seen and heard moving on the right and left flanks.'[43]

The force was now effectively encircled and captive on this small beach behind enemy lines with no obvious avenue of recovery.

The reserves of ammunition, now isolated on the grounded supply barge on the reef, were vital to the success of this operation and the inability to salvage them was a serious concern. As Major Dick Sampson later observed,

> 'Loss of supply was to be one of the deciding factors in the outcome of this battle'.

Without access to their ammunition the Australians' situation began to deteriorate rapidly.

[43] *At War with the 31/51st Infantry Battalion*, Major W.E. Hughes MBE RL, Church Archivist Press, 1993, p230. Report written on the 24 June 1945 by Sergeant G. Tickle, Commander of 9 Section, 9 Platoon.

Friday, June 8 – Day 1

Digging In 8

As the men of the [second wave] 14 Platoon "C" Company were establishing their perimeter and digging in, Captain Blue Shilton assessed the situation:

> 'Half the perimeter was among the trees but the rear half was completely without cover. Movement was very difficult, dangerous, and became more so when the Japs set up a position near the jetty. Siting of the RAP [Regimental Aid Post] was a problem as the only suitable spot had no shade at all for the wounded who soon flowed in. I tried several times to unload the stores barge but machine-gun fire would have seen all the troops lost as they would have been visible in the water for about 75 metres. It was a case of a line of men in the water and you'd pass the stores down the line but in the end we wouldn't have had any men or stores – they would all have been killed.'

It was impossible to establish the Regimental Aid Post on the beach with the usual stretchers, tent, facilities, drugs and dressings, because those things were also on the stranded stores barge. Without the essential equipment and supplies the frustrated 19th Field Ambulance medical personnel were severely hampered in their attempts to minister to the casualties which increased rapidly as the battle progressed.

The orderlies described how during the action the lesser wounded remained in weapon-pits and trenches with their mates. The seriously injured, retrieved at great risk by stretcher-bearers (with no stretchers) from the place where they fell, were deposited in the only available area on that beach - in shallow pits under the scorching tropical sun. Later, during periodic lulls in the firing, it was sometimes possible to take them further up the beach to Company Headquarters where there was sparse shade at the edge of the plantation.

The Medical Officer and ambulance personnel, under constant heavy fire, were forced to crawl from their adjacent pits to attend to the men's wounds, give them water as necessary and provide whatever basic emergency care was possible in the absence of proper medical supplies. Badly wounded troops were positioned closest to the water's edge on the foreshore in order to be withdrawn first should evacuation become necessary.

One of the ambulance orderlies recalled the section's anger and frustration at this situation:

> 'We had very experienced and battle-hardened medical people at Porton, a team which unfortunately never performed the duties they were sent there for – and that applies to the whole miserable affair. We just had to do the best we could with the limited facilities we had. One man's broken leg was splinted with his gun which was held in place by his torn-up shirt.'

The 15 medical orderlies from the 19th Field Ambulance who landed at Porton suffered heavy casualties with three killed, two missing and eight wounded.

Although wireless communication with the gunners at 4 Field Regiment 8 kilometres away on Soraken Peninsula, was achieved by 5.00 a.m., and effective artillery fire brought down on the enemy by 6.12 a.m., the continuous Japanese gunfire made any future communication or movement between pits almost impossible. Therefore when it became necessary for Blue Shilton to contact the C.O. he had to brave the fire,

> '….and crawl up [the beach] to Clyde Downs [at Company Headquarters] a couple of times to alert him to our problems [retrieving the stores]. He virtually only had a shallow scrape in the predominantly coral swamp affording very little protection.'

There were many individual acts of heroism in the hours which followed. Vickers gunner the late Corporal Felix Grasso was one of many men who faced flying bullets and shrapnel in order to help a mate in trouble. Without hesitation he left his trench to take water to patrol member Lloyd Burke who lay badly wounded and exposed to the hot sun in a nearby bomb crater. Felix then escorted the Medical Officer to Burke's position to administer a pain-killing injection. Sadly, Lloyd Burke died of his wounds before he could be returned to the perimeter.

It was predictable that the survivors' first impressions of Porton were brief as the men landed and rushed to dig their pits, the men of the second wave making themselves as safe as possible while under the murderous hail of Japanese gunfire. Digging-in in this coastal terrain of coral rock and swamp was both slow and laborious. In places the water-table was only about 35 centimetres below ground and newly-dug weapon pits rapidly began to fill with evil-smelling swamp water.

Private Don Schapel recalls:

> 'We dug our pits but because we were digging in a swamp we had to bail the pit out every so often.

When the Jap machine-guns opened up we were in our pits like rabbits in a burrow'.

Lieut. K. Scoble O.C.
A.A.S.C Porton, June 1945
Bougainville.

Lieutenant Keith Scoble of the Army Service Corps wrote:

'At 4.35 am after wading ashore from the second wave of grounded landing craft the men of the ASC detachment consisting of 6 other ranks and myself, were under fire but managed to gain their position [on the left flank] without casualty. In this area, 30 metres from the beach, it was swampy with thick secondary growth and digging-in was difficult owing to the coral rock. However, by first light all personnel were in position and stood to.'

He later recalled how, after many hours sitting or crouching in the water in these pits, he and his men found their situation was becoming unbearable:

'By now the stinking swamp water had risen to shoulder height, making conditions unpleasant. Sitting immersed in the pits for so long had cramped most of us and relief was sought by stretching out for a few minutes under salt scrub within the perimeter. We were fired at by a hidden sniper, the bullet hitting Private Jennings as it ricocheted away, inflicting a slight flesh wound.

Any movement outside our pits immediately drew fire.'

Lieutenant Blue Reiter wryly observed, 'It was either get shot in a shallow hole or get drowned digging deeper.'

Corporal H. Tymms was also one of the A.S.C. detachment who crouched in their swampy pits as enemy fire and 4 Field Regiment artillery shells passed close over their heads. He has never forgotten the shattering noise and the nearness of the attack – the roar of low-flying aircraft, whine of shells and the thunderous blast of the exploding bombs dropped by the Royal New Zealand Air Force Corsairs:

'The FOO [Forward Observation Officer] was situated right next to us directing the arty on to the targets. Shells could be plainly heard screaming over; those that fell in the sea sent up huge volumes of water as they exploded. TacR aircraft circled overhead most of the morning and later the Corsairs unloaded their bombs outside the perimeter. The noise was unbelievable.'

After landing from the first wave of barges that reached Porton, Private (Stiffy) Flynn of 8 Platoon quickly discovered the difficulties involved in trying to dig-in with a bayonet instead of the usual trenching tool. His comments also highlight how isolated the men were from one another, all confined in their own separate pits by the ferocity of enemy fire:

'Our platoon occupied the east and south of the perimeter and I was never to see what was happening in the northern area. We dug, or tried to dig, our weapon-pits but the ground was so hard we were lucky to make a depression of about forty-five centimetres. Bayonets were our only digging implements.

'When we could dig no further we heaped lumps of coral around our pits to add a little more protection. I put a watermelon-size piece of coral behind my head to protect my rear as we were on slightly higher ground and fire which was coming across from the other side ploughed into our area. When I left my pit that watermelon was more like a large grapefruit. At around mid-day I tried to boil my little billy (on canned heat); twice they knocked it over and the third time they put a hole in it!'

One man commented:

'Crouching in our pits we could see nothing. Put your head up and you immediately become a prime target.'

Private Viv Taylor 19 Field Ambulance was in the first wave of landings. He was later to have a dramatic rescue from the sea. There was a touch of farce in the colourful memories of the Porton landing which remained with him:

'I think we were the first barge ashore and not a shot had been fired. By the time the Japs opened up with their barrage of automatic fire most of us had trenches dug. It was all close combat and I can still hear the impact of bullets hitting human flesh. I remember a fellow in a trench near my mate Welshie and me letting out a hell of a yell of agony and using much profanity. His mate said with great concern, "Where did he hit you mate?" and he replied, "In the bloody arse!" so loud that every Jap must have heard. I lay in bed at night and think of that episode because it was the only incident at Porton that made me smile. Sad.'

Private Merv Porter of 8 Platoon was another one of the first wave fortunate to have reached the beach before the shooting began. He recalls:

'We dug in thankful there had been no opposition. Our holes filled with water when the tide came in. The Japs knew we were there after the supply barge got stuck on the reef and kicked up an awful racket trying to get off. At daylight we moved into thick vegetation on our right flank and found the Japs were there ahead of us.

'We discovered the fresh-water hole about 20-30 metres from the beach when Ron Codrington fell into it. This waterhole appeared to be an old bomb crater, probably from a bomb dropped earlier by the Americans. There was a two - wheel track nearby and we thought it was maybe the Jap water supply because they later tried to reclaim it. After we engaged the enemy, night and day just seemed to blend into one another.'

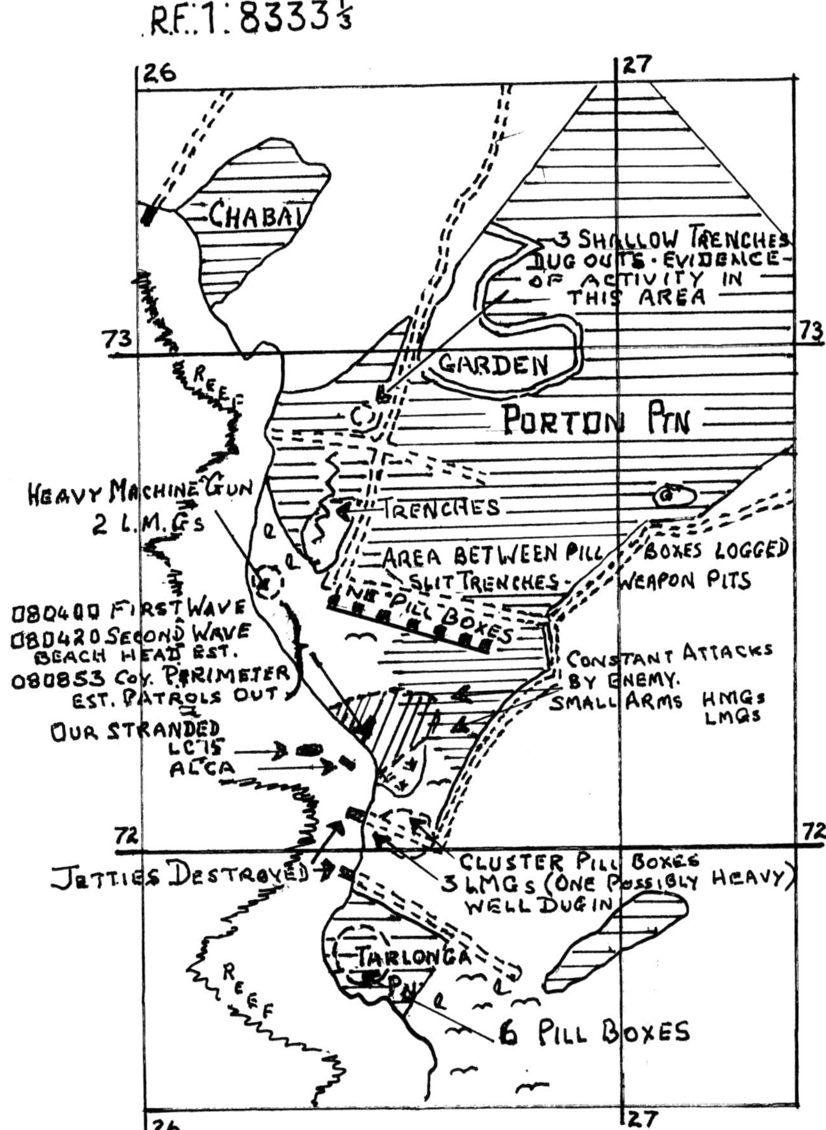

ENLARGEMENT: PORTON AREA
Ref map: Chabai 1:25,000

Friday, June 8

The First Day 9

At 5.10 a.m. Captain Downs held a conference with his platoon leaders prior to sending out reconnaissance patrols to establish the strength and disposition of the enemy's defences. These patrols quickly confirmed a significant Japanese presence in every landward direction. As 4th Field Regiment artillery fire from the Soraken battery began to strip the trees and scythe through the undergrowth the formidable line of stoutly constructed pill-boxes and trenches was revealed, arranged in a cordon around the beach area. These defences had been observed and accurately reported on by TacR aircraft before the battle.[44]

The Japs had made their pill-boxes almost impregnable. Earth-filled metal drums protected the gunners inside from shrapnel. They laid coconut tree logs across the front and sides and over the top of their dugouts and a slit along the front allowed them to shoot at invaders with rifles or machine guns. This made them safe from any but a lucky direct shot or well-aimed grenade or bomb; it also made them very difficult to eradicate, as the seemingly indestructible fortifications at the jetty site were later to prove.

Lieutenant Reiter's 9 Platoon occupied the forward line in the assault perimeter. Following the platoon conference he observed:

> 'Captain Downs stated we would hold the position to protect the stores barge until it could be

[44] *At War with the 31/51st Infantry Battalion,* Major W.E. Hughes MBE RL, Church Archivist Press, 1993, p210

> unloaded. He ordered 9 Platoon to push a patrol forward at first light. I was in charge of three of these patrols and, with Jap pressures on our front, the last one only got about 100 metres out. Sergeant Cullen's No. 2 patrol departed at 7.45 a.m. and pushed forward 200 metres into Porton Plantation. After hearing and seeing enemy movement, the patrol tried to outflank them but in doing this another Japanese force was sighted.
>
> 'We found Japanese defence positions 60 metres apart. The patrol also tried to outflank them but due to the openness of the country we were unable to attack without serious casualties. The patrol moved 400 to 500 metres along the enemy defensive line and killed one Japanese. Four rifles opened fire from two positions, without inflicting casualties, so we returned to the perimeter.'

At this early stage the troops had already observed Japanese reinforcements moving overland from their large garrison on Buka Island 18 kilometres to the north. With external resources no longer available to them, the existing enemy force of 100 men at Porton had rapidly deployed troops from the surrounding area and Buka when the Australians landed at the beach. Their snipers quickly took up positions in the surrounding trees and during the battle were responsible for many casualties among the assault force. When a sniper was shot another immediately took his place.

Japanese author Seiji Hondo, a survivor of the Bonis Peninsula conflict wrote after the war:

> 'Whatever happened, they [the Australians] would have to be stopped at Porton. The Porton battle was truly the battle on which the fate of Buka Island hung.'[45]

The Japanese reinforcement troops from Buka belonged to the elite Imperial Naval Force. Ex-2/8th Commando Squadron author Peter Pinney described these men in his *Solomon Islands War Diary, 1945:*

> 'Japanese naval fighters, trained by the British, are the Emperor's crack troops. Big men, many of them, clad in naval grey.....they were older men, seasoned veterans.'[46]

Gavin Long in *The Final Campaigns* noted:

> 'It was evident that the Japanese Naval Force was resolute, enterprising and skilful and that any gain by Australians would be bought only at the cost of hard fighting.'[47]

A Japanese report later showed that an attack in this area had been anticipated for some time and naval troops had been waiting at Buka ready to occupy the prepared defences at Porton when needed. It was becoming increasingly obvious that the reports of an enemy build-up in this area, though disregarded by Brigade, had been dangerously accurate.

[45] *Solomon No Gyokuswbutai*, Seiji Honda, translated by Prof Alan Rix, p357

[46] *Devils' Garden. Solomon Islands War Diary, 1945,* Peter Pinney, UQP p47

[47] *At War with the 31/51st Infantry Battalion,* Major W.E.Hughes MBE RL, Church Archivist Press, 1993, p206

Captain Downs ordered patrols to go out to the north, south and east of the beachhead perimeter. The fighting patrols of Lieutenant Reiter's 9 Platoon in the eastern sector quickly located and engaged groups of the enemy, killing several and wounding many others. Private John Goodchild of 9 Platoon, who was wounded in later action, was on one of these patrols led by Corporal Garth Tickle. He recalled:

> 'Around 800 metres out [from the perimeter] we saw enemy troops moving towards us and we quickly set up an ambush. That first engagement was short-lived but very intense and we retired to the safety of our own perimeter. Later that morning we again moved out about 400 metres on that same track to establish a listening post. We saw enemy troops approaching and we opened fire on them with our Owen guns. They immediately returned fire and we quickly realized they were a strong force. When their fire weakened we withdrew.'

Patrols by 8 Platoon led by Lieutenant Bill Evans, and 7 Platoon commanded by Lieutenant Noel Smith, also went into operation at that time to the north and south of the beachhead. The 8 Platoon patrol reconnoitred the jetty area and they noted:

> 'One and possibly two pill-boxes were sighted east and south of the northern jetty. Several Japanese were sighted moving towards the pill-boxes from the south. One Jap was killed.'[48]

Lieutenant Smith and his 7 Platoon patrol departed to

[48] 31/51st Australian Infantry Battalion Confidential Report, p30

silence the heavy machine-gun position to the north-west of the beachhead. They engaged groups of Japanese, killing two. Three members of the patrol became separated from the others after an enemy ambush but were unable to return to their perimeter until seven hours later because of the large numbers of the enemy in the surrounding area and the severity of their fire.

Lieutenant Smith and the rest of the patrol were still missing. However, next day two more members of the patrol, without a compass, managed to make their way to Ratsua after a perilous trek through thick jungle; they reported that Lieutenant Smith had been badly wounded in the arm and was unable to be moved. Unwilling to jeopardise the safety of the remaining group he had instructed the two men to leave him and go to Ratsua to bring back help if possible.

By this time Smith was becoming delirious from pain and loss of blood and his loyal batman, Private E. M. Duck, stayed by his side. After the troops who went for help eventually reached Ratsua they attempted to lead a rescue party back to the wounded man. However they became completely disoriented in the jungle and despite hours of frantic searching, were unable to find the place where they had last seen Lieutenant Smith and Private Duck.

Noel Smith and his batman perished in that jungle wilderness so dense that their bodies were never found.[49] The full extent of the pain and terror endured by the dying man and his companion in those endless dark hours as they watched and waited for the rescuers who failed to return, can never be known. It is certain however that their anguish was only a part of the huge burden of needless suffering

[49] *At War with the 31/51st Infantry Battalion,* Major W.E. Hughes MBE RL, Church Archivist Press, 1993, p251

endured by Australian servicemen who fought in those final, futile, Pacific campaigns.

After the landing at Porton beach the men in Mortar Platoons found themselves in the thick of the action without their weapons. Intense enemy automatic fire persisted in the area of the stores barge so that the heavy guns, bombs and ammunition supplies on board were unable to be salvaged by the troops. As a Mortar gunner attached to 14 Platoon "C" Company, Corporal Jerry Gehringer recalled his experience on that first morning:

> 'I was in charge of a 2 inch mortar at the time and I landed with only a revolver, 6 rounds of ammo and 2 hand grenades. The mortars and bombs, together with other equipment, were on the supply barge stranded on the reef. We were given little notice or preparation for the landing at Porton. I was attached to 14 Platoon "C" Company under Captain Blue Shilton. We were told to get all our equipment ready and be prepared to leave by landing craft to take up a position further up the coast. We embarked on June 8 and when we reached Porton it was a case of making our way ashore and digging in. We were pinned down by the Japs and with all avenues cut off it was you and a mate holed up in a trench.'

Private Bill Aspinall belonged to a mortar platoon attached to "A" Company. He looked in vain for some protection on the beach after landing:

> 'My first thought that morning was to find a safe place – but not a lot was offering. I managed to find some soft sand and tried to dig myself in.

Bill Aspinall

But soon I could go no further and ended up behind a huge rock. I had a peep around it and saw two Japs preparing a machine gun. I had a grenade in my hand ready for use so I let them have it.

'I was in a mortar platoon attached to "A" Company but we were unable to operate because the mortars were on the stores barge. The Japs had their pill-boxes on a nearby rise and we were just sitting ducks. However, it wasn't until the New Zealand Corsairs supported us later on by bombing their defences, that I got some shrapnel in my knee.'

The troops all had three days' field rations with them – bully beef, cooked rice and army biscuits, and they also carried emergency rations and a water bottle. They recalled that the first day was cloudless and sweltering under the tropical sun. There was little chance to eat or rest - or refill their water bottles except at great risk at the waterhole. This was also the Japanese fresh water supply and therefore heavily contested by them.

During the morning of that first day Japanese attacks were maintained and they steadily increased in intensity throughout the day.

'Pressure began to be exerted on the perimeter from the north and east, whilst the southern flank was being harassed by automatics. Patrols sent from the Company found great difficulty in returning; in several cases the enemy had worked his way in to

> encircle the perimeter. At 1.40 p.m. pressure from the south was felt when two automatic weapons opened up from approximately 100 metres south of the north jetty.'[50]

Since 6.45 a.m. TacR low-flying Boomerang aircraft had been directing artillery fire onto enemy gun positions, and later they pinpointed targets for the R.N.Z.A.F. Corsairs to bomb and strafe. The sustained and co-ordinated teamwork of all supporting units in this battle during the next seventy-two hours was remarkable. Artillery, airforce, engineers, water transport, ambulance, signals and supplies – the integrated support of all these services meant that the troops had a fighting chance of survival at times when it seemed certain their perimeter was about to be completely overrun by the enemy.

However, it was the pin-point accuracy of artillery shelling from Soraken which all survivors remembered with awe and gratitude. The 4th Field Regiment [Jungle Division] Forward Observation Officer was Lieutenant D.F. Spark M.C. who, like Major Dick Sampson, Captain Blue Shilton and Lieutenant Blue Reiter, was a 6th Division veteran of the Middle East campaigns. He had been imprisoned with Blue Reiter after the fall of Crete, escaped with him in the stolen fishing boat, and was rescued later by a British submarine. At Porton Blue was amazed to meet him again:

> 'I heard a voice asking for the OC of the platoon. I knew that voice! I turned around and said, "What the hell are you doing here?" He stated that I took the words out of his mouth'.

[50] War Diary of 31/51st Australian Infantry Battalion.

The 4th Field Regiment had previously fought alongside the 31/51 Battalion and they had developed a firm bond of trust. Lieutenant Spark made out an excellent fire plan for Porton which he gave in detail in the report of his unit's action at Porton.

His report also described how, after the barges reached Porton in the second wave of the landing, the men had difficulty moving their equipment,

> '…carrying such heavy articles as No. 11 Set and accumulators at a high level out of the water. As the landing was made north of the correct spot, land marks which indicated the positions of groups were not available. The most disturbing discovery was the fact that there were no trees in the immediate vicinity which could be used for the wireless aerial. The FOO went forward with a runner from Company Headquarters to contact the Company Commander. Owing to the difficulty of erecting an aerial, communications were not established until 6.01a.m.'

AWM092782. Members of E Troop, 12 Battery, manning No.4 gun on Soraken Peninsula. This was one of the guns which fired on Japanese positions on Porton

Machine gun targets were registered on the north and the south flank where further automatics were suspected to be dug in. Lieutenant Spark, who had joined Captain Downs at Company Headquarters, continued his report:

> 'At the northern jetty on the south flank, on the shore, was a large clump of trees. The Company Commander Captain Downs suspected that automatic weapons may have been sited there. The timber at the base was about 4 – 5metres thick with a multitude of sparse limbs some of which overhung the water's edge. Fire when called upon was most accurate on this point, all rounds fired hitting some part of this bulky piece of timber. Sometime later automatic fire came from this site and when Artillery was brought to bear on it, the fire either ceased or was spasmodic. Even with one gun so accurately registered onto the point, continuous firing would never have knocked it out. Had sufficient ammunition been available the post could have been silenced until further notice.'

The earliest reports had noted that this jetty area was a focus of enemy strength. Following Artillery's failed attempts to knock out the seemingly indestructible line of pill-boxes which had been strategically placed to guard the jetty, the subsequent bombing and strafing by Royal New Zealand Air Force Corsairs had also been unsuccessful in dislodging them. Japanese reserve troops coming down from Buka kept those guns manned and firing, inflicting serious injuries on the Australian lines. They also prevented the grounded supply barge being unloaded and they blocked the landing of further supplies at the jetty site.

Major Dick Sampson and beachmaster Captain Blue

Shilton thought that, in order to gain control of the landing site for future resupply, the Company's perimeter should be extended to include the strongly defended jetty area. Their reports clearly indicated that the precarious state of the ammunition supply had become a primary concern for all the Commanders.

There was obvious uncertainty about the will or ability of Brigade to resupply the force, and in addition there was a strong probability that weapons and ammunition stores on the supply barge would prove irretrievable. In the absence of heavy weapons, and lacking an assured resupply of ammunition, Captain Downs as C.O. of the assault force decided it would be unwise to commit his small Company of men to such a perilous attack. It did not go ahead.

At 8.00 a.m. on June 8 Tac HQ received a signal from Captain Downs:

> 'Unable to get stores from stranded barge STOP Have no 2 inch or 3 inch mortars and have no reserve ammo STOP Request arrange dropping suitable position available in swamp at 265 722 STOP Stores required SAA charger carton and 9mm grenades 4-Sec Sigcable and 2 days rations STOP Advise if can be arranged and time STOP Will attempt to offload barge tonight.'

On receipt of this signal TacHQ requested an air drop but this was rejected by Corps in Torokina.[51]

During the first day even the inspired shelling by 4th Field Regiment at Soraken failed to prevent the Japanese constantly raking the beach and stores barge with heavy

[51] *At War with the 31/51st Infantry Battalion*, Major W.E. Hughes MBE RL, Church Archivist Press, 1993, p215

automatic fire. No supplies were rescued from the stores barge during daylight and another attempt was planned for the night of June 8.

According to the original battle plan the heavily defended jetty was the proposed site for the landing that night of another platoon of "C" Company together with supplies of ammunition and stores. Following this plan TacHQ made arrangements for the operation to go ahead at 8.00 p.m. However, "A" Company advised them at 8.15 a.m. that it was now too dangerous to attempt to land here as the enemy had enfiladed all the jetty area. Despite the warning, TacHQ decided to adhere to the original plan and rely on its own firepower and Artillery shelling to cover the landing. "A" Company suggested that an alternative landing site or an airdrop next morning might be more practicable but there was no change of plan.[52]

The Australian attacking force was reduced to a defending force by 1 p.m. as Japanese pressure continued to grow. Artillery's observation post on Taiof Island reported enemy barges moving through the Buka passage from Buka to Bonis at the northern tip of Bougainville. During the afternoon transport vehicles could be heard bringing in these enemy troops from the north. Fire was now being exchanged at very short range. Three Japanese with a light machine-gun crawled to within ten metres of Private Ward's pit in the 7 Platoon sector of the perimeter and commenced firing into the perimeter:

> 'Ward promptly threw a grenade and, despite the intensity of the enemy automatic and small arms fire in the area, jumped out of his pit and rushed

[52] 31/51st Australian Infantry Battalion (AIF) Confidential Report, p31

> forward shooting the 3 Japanese with his rifle and knocked out the LMG. Four other Japanese promptly attacked him from a flank. He shot one, then taking cover, killed the other 3 by rifle fire.'[53]

By 6 p.m. 50mm mortar fire was coming against the Australians' perimeter from the north and from the direction of the fresh waterhole which lay between 7 Platoon and 9 Platoon. There were 8 casualties here including 1 man killed, 1 officer and 6 other ranks missing. The attacks intensified and concentrated heavy fire now poured in from all directions with an estimated 12 – 15 automatics firing at once.

The noise was shattering. The whip and crack of gunfire, scream of shells and the shuddering blast of detonating grenades and mortars rose in a mind-numbing crescendo of violence. As shells exploded against tree trunks the air was heavy with smoke and dust and shrapnel. Among flying shards of steel the finely-shredded vegetation drifted down and settled on the troops' heads and shoulders as they crouched in their flooded weapon pits. The detritus covered their hands which held the guns and it covered their wounds. During those hours the whole world seemed to lie under a pall of destruction and fright.

If it were possible at that time for men to raise their heads briefly to look over their shoulders for a just moment they would have seen, in the west beyond the gunsmoke and desolation, that the sea was a serene vision of space and

[53] Private Kenneth Robert Ward's citation for the award of D.C.M.

light and shimmering water. Reflecting the last rays of the setting sun it shone like burnished brass, a timely reminder of normality and peace.

The enemy bombardment continued into the night and there was no rest. John Goodchild had grim memories of the death of his friend during that first night:

> 'Darkness brought no respite, enemy harassment increased, and our casualties mounted. My good friend Sam Salmon was badly wounded by machine-gun fire in the late evening and died of his wounds that night.'

During lulls in the firing there were sounds of stealthy movement in the eerie darkness around the perimeter. It seemed that the unseen enemy was all around, a felt presence. The crouching troops watched and listened tensely all night, never relaxing vigilance for a moment. Porton was Corporal Eric Hall's first experience of front-line action. After Merauke he had been diverted into Army training courses and clerical duties at Warwick and Canungra, and he had not rejoined his unit until May 30 1945. Eric described his first night of action as "a night of terror" as the Japanese crept furtively about attempting to invade the men's pits.

Ambulanceman Viv Taylor and his mate had a contingency plan in case the worst happened. Viv describes the horror of those dark hours:

> 'I can still hear the night-long trauma of mortars at close range and, in the breaks of fire, the taunts of the Japs who had infiltrated the perimeter in darkness. My mate Welshie and I decided that if they jumped into our trench we would pull the

pin of a grenade and at least take them with us. This was mainly because we had seen in previous battles down the coast some of the terrible wounds inflicted on our troops when the Japs jumped into the trenches with them, madly striking with their swords.'

Pte. Dick Welsh and Pte. Viv Taylor

Stretcher-bearer Dick Welsh was the mate who shared Viv Taylor's trench and he also anticipated the worst:

'We were dug in so close to Japanese pill-boxes you were frightened to put your head up or it would be blown off. All through the day there were clashes and Viv and I copped plenty. All through the night the Japs would crawl around saying, "Is there any room in there, Bill?" I said to Viv, "This is it mate, I think we are going to the mansion in the sky." Later in the night I remember Captain Downs coming down to see if we were all right. Being stretcher-bearers we were not trained for that type of fighting, but I can remember him saying,

"Hang on boys, you are doing a great job."'

Gunner Gordon (Deena) McHugh's pit was close to a mangrove swamp and in *The Savage Shore* he spoke of hearing weird noises throughout that first fearful night:

> 'It was amazing the way the crabs were going "crack, crack, crack " all night. I didn't know what they were, and none of us knew if they were the

Two Corsair bombers of the RNZAF have just completed a bombing run over the Japanese positions and the white smoke of the bomb bursts are discernible. Smoke from the battlefield obliterates half of the featureless beach at Porton. This shot taken from one of the barges lying out to sea out of range of small arms fire.

> Nips sneaking in – or what they were. They didn't help the nerves at all!'

At 8.40 p.m. another signal from Captain Downs to TacHQ had reported that the enemy was continuing to bear down on the perimeter with increasing automatic and mortar fire. The message stated that as the shortage of ammunition had become acute it would not be possible for the force to clear the Japanese machine-gun positions at the jetty, which had been requested by TacHQ. These guns covered the proposed landing point for the supply barges coming in that night so any landing would be heavily contested.

Regardless of this signal, preparations for the landing proceeded. The 15 Platoon of "C" Company and a detachment of flamethrowers and signallers, together with stores, were to be brought ashore in five landing craft at 9.00 p.m. under the supervision of Major Dick Sampson. Another attempt was to be made to unload the stores barge at the same time.[54]

As the flotilla departed from Soraken heavy fire could be heard at Porton 8 kilometres away. A fierce firefight was already under way there as the first two barges approached the dark beach where a beach light had been displayed to guide them in. However, notwithstanding their own fire and excellent support from Artillery it was impossible for the Landing Craft crew to bring their barges in through the heavy curtain of fire. Captain Leslie ordered the craft to withdraw and the attempt was abandoned.[55]

Since resupply of ammunition was now deemed crucial to the survival of the force, Major Sampson made another attempt to land at 2.00 a.m. on the same night. Once again, the craft were repulsed by the strength of the enemy's defences. He describes the event:

> 'When still 200 – 300 metres from the beach the leading ALCA was subjected to heavy fire, small arms and heavier, from several points north and

[54] *At War with the 31'51st Infantry Battalion*, Major W.E. Hughes MBE RL, Church Archivist Press, 1993, p216

[55] *The Final Campaigns*, Gavin Long. p212

south of the landing point. A heavy belt of fire was falling in front of the ALCA and all attempts to land the troops and stores were abandoned. The stranded LC15 was subjected to heavy gun fire every time the enemy suspected activity near it.'

The barges again withdrew to base.

Lieutenant Sparks reported on the looming crisis in Artillery's ammunition supply:

'Throughout the night there was considerable activity in the way of grenades thrown into the perimeter, also some small arms fire. Little could be done about it with artillery. In view of the ammunition state no shooting was done till next morning.'

For Signaller Bill Hughes it was a long dark night:

'At about 9.21 p.m. 8 Section of 9 Platoon suffered casualties from grenades. Corporal Doug (Donkey) Seymour carried them back to Company Headquarters and requested two volunteers from Headquarters Company personnel to take their place in the weapon pits. Fred Stamp and I volunteered. It was extremely dark and nothing could be seen. Although I did not look forward to the dawn attack, I longed for daylight so I could see what was happening around me.'

Because of the recurring Japanese attacks it was a sleepless and nerve-racking night for all the troops in their pits. They had held the enemy off strenuously but in the early hours of June 9 trucks could be heard bringing more Japanese reinforcements from Buka. Their force was now estimated at 400 – 500 men and it was evident that they were about to mount a major assault on the Australian line. The Australian losses after 24 hours had been slight - with four killed and seven wounded. This was because the perimeter had been established before the firing began, and also because the enemy fire had been wild and inaccurate.

Captain Shilton stated that he had never before experienced such intense automatic fire as he saw at Porton. War correspondent Chester Wilmot wrote of the "noise tactics" which were being employed by the attacking Japanese in New Guinea:

> 'They shouted like Red Indians and frequently fired their automatic rifles and machine-guns at random for morale effect. By shouting and random firing, half a dozen Japs in the jungle.... often seemed like half a hundred.'[56]

For the Australians "the failure to land supplies and ammunition at Porton [the previous night] influenced the issues from that time forward".[57]The implications of that failure were not lost on the troops. It is obvious from the accounts of the battered and weary men who had been trapped for 24 hours in their swampy pits, that they believed the approaching day brought them no promise of reprieve. Their reports of that time reflected increasing urgency and alarm as their ammunition supply dried up and enemy numbers more than trebled. They began to realize that as a force they might be facing extinction.

The major Japanese assault came at first light. They fired into the perimeter from all directions and attacked in

[56] *Chester Wilmot Reports*, Neil McDonald, ABC Books, 2004, p327

[57] War Diary of the 31/51st Australin Infantry Battalion, p4

waves.[58] As they were driven off others took their place. Captain Shilton reported on the urgent redistribution of men and ammunition within the force to meet this attack:

> 'At dawn on June 9 the Japs increased their attacks still more and the wounded mounted up. Ammunition was collected from the rear troops and taken forward. Men were taken from 14 Platoon, Bill Evans' platoon [7 Platoon], mortarmen and others, to reinforce the "A" Company platoons which were having it very tough. Once again Clyde's [Downs] request for an ammo drop was refused by Brigade. They stated they thought we had enough. Typical of the paper-shufflers with no respect for the man in charge or the troops.'

Private Goodchild was well aware of the developing situation:

> 'The coming of daylight saw attacks launched on all sides of the perimeter as the enemy quickly realized that we were cut off from supplies and were rapidly exhausting our ammunition. Only the constant artillery fire from 4th Field Regiment and accurate bombing by the R.N.Z.A.F. Corsairs prevented us being overrun early in the day.'

By mid-morning there was a lull in the fighting and forward troops were temporarily relieved by Headquarters men. The forward troops were exhausted from lack of sleep and unrelieved tension as the Japs continued their relentless attacks and determined attempts to infiltrate the Australian perimeter.

[58] War Diary of the 31/51st Australin Infantry Battalion, p5

Ambulanceman Viv Taylor recalls his reluctance when asked to give up his precious ammunition:

'Our medical people were never trained for combat but before leaving Soraken we had been issued with a rifle and ammo and a belt full of hand grenades so most of us had an idea of what lay ahead of us. At Porton it was very hard to give our ammunition to a 31st/51st Battalion soldier who went around collecting it for the Vickers gunners but we knew it may be necessary for survival and knew they would use it well. So we were out of ammunition – but still had our rifles and bayonets and those lovely little pineapples [grenades]. We had many wounded and some shot up badly but refused to die, and I hope they are still alive and well today.

'We would have been easy pickings for the Japs except for that marvellous man called the OP [Forward Observation Officer] who was stationed near to our trench. We could hear him giving directions to the "five-mile snipers", the gunners of 4 Field Regiment artillery five miles away on Soraken Peninsula, and I think we would have been history without their support. They were dropping shells so close to us we thought they might make a mistake and drop one on us. And we could still hear the OP requesting the gunners to "bring them in closer". They were in my mind the reason the bloody Japs kept their heads down otherwise they would have overrun us long before'.

Saturday, June 9 – Day 2

10 Withdrawal

On the morning of June 9, with ammunition supplies depleted and large numbers of the enemy poised to broach the perimeter, it was decided by Brigade that there was no alternative but to withdraw the force that night as its position could not be maintained without heavy losses. The confidential report lists the messages which were sent and received in connection with the evacuation:

To "A" Company 8 a.m.

'16664 withdrawal tonight ALCAs will come in singly STOP troops will have to wade out due to low tide estimated time of arrival 10.00 p.m. STOP display beach light.'

From "A" Company 12.00 midday.

'Require ALCAs to withdraw rear troops immediately.'

To "A" Coy 12.15 p.m.

'Is point clear?'

From "A" Coy 12.25 p.m.

'Point is not clear STOP will require own fire support plus artillery.'

To "A" Coy 12.30 p.m.

'ALCAs on way have requested air strike.'

From "A" Coy 1.04 p.m.

'Ref your 1664 desire to commence 8.00 p.m. NOT repeat NOT 10.00 p.m. previously required STOP Find it very difficult to hold perimeter after dark.'

To "A" Coy 1.55 p.m.

'If possible evacuate whole force this afternoon STOP

personnel only STOP Barges will be standing by STOP air strike and air drop shortly.'

It was proposed that, under cover of bombing and strafing by R.N.Z.A.F. and R.A.A.F., together with shelling by artillery, barges were to evacuate the force. Word was passed around to expect the rescue barges.

Shortage of the ammunition necessary for 4th Field Regiment to support the evacuation remained a serious concern. Soon after 11.00 a.m. Captain Downs asked the Forward Observation Officer about the state of artillery's ammunition. Lieutenant Sparks reported:

'Signals followed:

11.24 a.m. Message to Battery from F.O.O. 'We are in a jam, would like C.O. to take up ammunition position with Brigadier.'

11.40 a.m Allotment of ammunition 700 rounds.

1.28 p.m. '900 rounds will be at your disposal.'

Sparks' report continued:

'At the gun end the ammunition was being unloaded from the barges on the beach and loaded practically straight into the breaches of the 12 hungry 25 pounders. All hands were on deck including the doctor, dentist, and their staffs. From about 10.00 a.m. on June 9 till the evacuation, guns were firing almost without a break. At this stage of the operation the situation looked particularly doubtful. At 3.00 p.m. the No. 11 wireless set was out of order. S.O.S was called three times by means of flares.'

Japanese harassment had continued all morning and at midday they launched another all-out attack. This was countered by Artillery's accurate shelling. The enemy attacked again at 1.00 p.m. bringing heavy mortar fire and grenades to bear against the perimeter. Aircraft returned and the enemy withdrew, but they resumed the attack every time the Boomerangs and Corsairs returned to Piva airfield near Torakina to bomb-up and refuel.

AWM078850. Common in the swampy areas of Bougainville water filled weapon pits like added to the difficulties at Porton.

For over 24 hours the intense enemy fire had kept the troops trapped in their weapon pits, unable to venture out for even a minute. While they might escape being hit by a sniper's bullet or a grenade there was no escape from the foul water in which they had been forced to stand or sit for so long. Beneath the sweltering sun everything was wet and stank of swamps and decay, and worse.

The heat was thick and heavy. Sweat poured down faces and stung eyes raw from gunsmoke and lack of sleep. It drenched the shirts which clung to bodies that itched and ached, cramped from fatigue and immobility. In the foetid swamp water the drag and chafe of sodden jungle greens on parts of the body which, after six months of jungle fighting were already scoured by flaring tinea and nameless tropical rashes, was excruciating. Feet squelched and sucked inside water-logged boots and legs were numb.

Lieutenant Keith Scoble recalls that second morning in the weapon pits of his ASC sector:

> 'As the morning passed it became obvious, despite the excellent support given by the Arty and the R.N.Z.A.F., that we must evacuate or be annihilated by the Japs' overwhelming numbers and tremendous firepower. The news that ALCAs were coming to evacuate our force was a great boost to morale. By early afternoon the attacks had reached fanatical intensity. Our sector was subjected to rifle fire from hidden snipers making it impossible to raise one's head, except for hurried observation, without being subjected to fire. Conditions in the pits were now almost unbearable. Eating, drinking and movement were impossible, personnel were cramped from lack of movement and the continued immersion in swamp water, and the sun heated our rifles until they were almost too hot to handle.'

The Japanese were attacking the perimeter from the north and east using mortars and grenades as well as MMGs and LMGs. Deadly debris was flying in every direction, flaying and tearing and stabbing at vegetation and human flesh. The landscape was desolate and shattered trees were stripped of their branches. Official photographs taken at that time show gaunt, bare tree trunks reaching out of the smoky haze like bony fingers raised to heaven in supplication - to an avenging or a non-existent God?

Relentless enemy attacks caused many casualties and these were now accumulating in the positions occupied by 7 Platoon and 9 Platoon. Private Ward of 7 Platoon was in the middle of the action:

> ‘There were at least 8 LMGs to our front and they were also throwing grenades – most Australian type 36s. Grenade dischargers were used continuously. Many determined enemy rushes were broken up by our grenades and arty fire. I was on the Bren team and there was an enemy LMG straight in front us. The arty failed to dislodge this one but we got them with a phosphorous grenade. My rifle was shot out of my hands and I took over the Bren whilst my mate [Pat Conroy] rested. He was later killed in the evacuation.
>
> ‘No orders had reached us regarding withdrawal and about 15 Japs poured through the gap left by troops on the right – I got five of them with the Bren.’

Inside the 9 Platoon perimeter the situation was looking very grave. Platoon commander Lieutenant Reiter reported:

> ‘From midday parties of Japs tried to overrun our position and numbers of them were killed or wounded. The platoon was unable to use the grenade launcher again because of shortage of ballistite cartridges. 7 Platoon was plastered with

grenades, mortars and a variety of machine guns. At 2.00 p.m. Captain Downs told me that 7 Platoon had been severely mortared so he was withdrawing them. He told me to withdraw 9 Platoon also to the new perimeter near the beach. Captain Downs with Captain Shilton directed the Sections into their new positions.'

Private Merv Porter of 8 Platoon remembers the dramatic commencement of the withdrawal:

'Things are a bit blurred now fifty-nine years later, but what is still quite clear is Captain Downs standing out in the open and calling out, "Fall back 7 Platoon, fall back 9 Platoon. Every man for himself!" Then I could see all these people running to the beach and I could not believe what was happening. Ron Codrington appeared out of the scrub near me and said, "We had better get out of here", so we headed for the beach too.'

By approximately 2.00 p.m. "A" Company, unable to hold the Japanese numbers, had pulled back to the beach and set up a new perimeter. The last of the ammunition had been issued. The Vickers gunners still had a little but this was used up in the last few minutes. There was great irony in the fact that Brigade had at last arranged the airdrop of supplies so long denied to Capt Downs and his men. This was to take place that afternoon but as the DC47 circled over Porton it was notified that the troops had been evacuated to the beach and the airdrop was cancelled.[59]

[59] 31/51st Australian Infantry Battalion (AIF), Confidential Report, p34

Signaller Bill Hughes recalled the withdrawal:

'I had half a magazine of ammunition left and knew that no more was available. In our haste to get to the new perimeter some pigeons were left in the cages. The sergeant at 14 Pigeon Loft would have been most upset to lose his birds. The Japanese probably ate them!

'The wounded and the dead were collected in a depression within the new perimeter, under the care of 19th Field Ambulance Orderlies, commanded by the Medical Officer, Captain Monaghan. I cannot recall ever seeing him. Perhaps I, like the others, was too busy trying to stay alive.'

The late Corporal Felix Grasso, one of Vickers gunners, is reputed to have been the last man to leave the beach after the rescue barges arrived. In his commentary which appeared in the documentary *The Savage Shore* Felix described the scene:

'We thought we'd get out under artillery fire – and then our right flank collapsed. I was on the left flank. Captain Downs came over to our gun and he said to me, "Keep your gun firing Corporal", which I did. When he said, "Righto cease firing, go for the barges" that's the time we stopped. But we kept firing till then and our Vickers machine-gun was that bloody hot you could hardly handle it.'

According to Lieutenant Blue Reiter,

'Captain Downs' plan of embarkation was to be in two waves but on withdrawing to the beach someone in charge of one of the barges yelled out

> "All come on board as we are not coming back" so there was a rush to board them. Because of this the barges were overloaded and they became grounded, stuck in the mud.'

By 1.45 p.m. the airstrike called for by TacHQ had commenced. R.A.A.F. Boomerang fighters "led in sixteen R.N.Z.A.F. Corsairs to strafe and bomb enemy positions. The aircraft each dropped 250 and 500 pound delayed action bombs on the old perimeter" [60]preventing the Japanese from occupying the area. Enemy gun positions which had been firing constantly onto the beach and seawards were also being bombed.

Artillery was bringing down precise fire to within 25metres of the troops on the beach. When the F.O.O. enquired whether the fire was too close he was told to "bring it a little closer". Suddenly the No.11 wireless went off the air. This meant that the only communication "A" Company had with Artillery after that time was by 208 wireless set through TacHQ. The next message received by TacHQ from "A" Company was from Signaller Wilbur Figg . It was short and graphic – "We are now on the beach and getting hell."[61] Captain Downs called for a heavy artillery barrage and gave the order to fix bayonets.

By 4.20 p.m. the 208 wireless set had also failed. All communication was now lost. The men were on their own. Rumour had it that the set was blasted out of Wilbur Figg's hand as he operated it.

The trees were full of Japanese snipers, especially in the jetty area. They were able to inflict severe casualties on the

[60] *At War with the 31/51st Infantry Battalion,* Major W.E. Hughes MBE RL, Church Archivist Press, 1993, p219

[61] Ibid. p5.

troops because they could fire directly down on the men as they reached their new beach perimeter. Lieutenant Blue Reiter recorded:

> 'After the 9th Platoon had been organized [near the jetty point] I reported to Captain Downs. He told me to set up the Vickers guns to fire against the snipers on our right. The enemy closed in and saturated the new perimeter with light machine-gun fire, sniper fire, grenades and mortars. I relocated our Vickers to give us more protection.'

Blue gave an ironic account of how luck was with him as they waited there for the rescue barges:

> 'When we were on the beach before embarking I was discussing the order of withdrawal with 2 I /C Captain Shilton when a Jap sniper opened fire. Blue [Shilton] got four or five bullets through the arm – and me alongside him not a scratch. Yelled for the Vickers near us "to spray that tree!" as there was a Jap in it. Corporal Felix Grasso was on the Vickers. On opening up, about twenty Japs fell out of it. It was like shaking a fruit tree and seeing all the apples hit the ground. So my luck held once again. Patched Blue up and told him to get going. They patched him up some more in Torokina'.

The confidential report observes that "The enemy's fanaticism prior to the evacuation was amazing. Regardless of losses they attacked in waves [of 8 – 12 men], only to be mown down by our fire".[62] This was despite the fact that

[62] 31/51st Australian Infantry Batalion Confidential Report, p34

the troops had been ordered to fire only at definite targets as they were using the last of the ammunition. It was estimated that at this stage the Japanese numbered 400-500 men.

To the battered and exhausted Australians who had no cover, no communications, depleted ammunition and supplies, a numerically superior enemy poised to overrun them and no rescue craft in sight, the situation could not have been more desperate. This was confirmed by the men themselves in their recollections of that day. In *The Savage Shore* Captain Blue Shilton's memory was clear as he recalled that critical time:

'In the finish we virtually ran out of ammunition and that's why we had to be evacuated. Sure, there were a few rounds left. I had one and I thought if the Japs were going to overrun us – bang! – because I knew what they would do. They were very keen, not using bullets they'd use a bayonet on anybody they got to, and I didn't fancy that really.'

LC 15 Barges.

ALCA (Australian Landing Craft Assault) Armoured Barge of the kind used at Porton,twin .303 Vickers MG aft and Browning MGs forward.

Saturday, June 9 – Day 2.

Evacuation 11

Stuart Leslie

The evacuation fleet of 3 ALCAs and 2 LC15s departed from Soraken at 3.30pm. Captain Leslie recalls that his barges were seriously unfit for this rescue operation:

'One of the ALCAs had commenced the journey with only one engine serviceable and Tommy Rose, who was in charge of the workshop section on Saposa Island, travelled with this craft with the engine partly dismantled. He somehow repaired it and had it operating by the time we reached the Porton beachhead.'

At 4.20 p.m. the rescue barges were seen approaching from Soraken. As they neared the beach the fearless Landing Craft crew led by Leslie was attempting to land the 3 ALCAs "with all guns blazing" through a hurricane of Japanese bullets. The barges charged in until they grounded on the reef 50 metres offshore. Two of the Vickers gunners were hanging dead in their harness and others had taken their place to keep the guns firing. In one of the outstanding acts of courage seen at Porton, ALCA gunner Sapper Harry Burrell, while waiting for ammunition for his Browning machine-gun to be replenished, "dashed along the catwalk fully exposed to enemy machine- gun fire to man the aft gun until it ran out of ammunition."[63] After that he returned to firing his Browning.

[63] Citation for the Award of MM to Sapper Harry Burrell

Two LC15s were positioned 400 to 600 metres further out at sea, exchanging fire with the enemy and prepared to receive the wounded from the beach as the ALCAs transferred them during the rescue.

Captain Leslie:

> 'The LC15s were thought to be sufficiently far out to avoid small arms fire but Corporal Bourke, an engineer on one of the craft, was killed. Sergeant Trainor who was in charge of that particular craft was also badly wounded by a bullet that passed through his lower face and jaw.'

Leslie had received orders that only two ALCAs were to be used for the evacuation and the third was to be reserved for General Blamey's use. At considerable risk to himself he decided that it was vital to have all three ALCAs available to the troops to achieve a rapid and successful withdrawal. He ignored Brigade's instructions and brought all the ALCAs in for the rescue. He was prepared to face the consequences.

As the ALCAs grounded offshore Captain Downs without hesitation gave the order the men had been waiting for – "GO FOR THE BARGES!" Those on the beach said it was only then that they realized an escape was actually possible. They saw that this was their only chance to get off ... to leave this hellhole...the murderous gunfire and the murdering hordes of Japanese...... to get aboard those waiting barges ...FAST .... and GO!

But, as the survivors also testified, to rush out and face that deadly hail of bullets seemed like suicide. Not to run meant a much worse fate back on the beach at the hands of the Japanese. They all knew of the barbaric treatment that was handed out to the wounded - and the enemy were taking no prisoners. Gunner Felix Grasso spoke of the terror of wounded and helpless men on the beach as they faced the possibility in those last desperate minutes that they might not be able to reach the rescue barges in time.

But for now the ALCAs were there, poised, ready. It was a powerful moment …. there were scant seconds left…. in a flash the stretcher-bearers deftly picked up the seriously wounded and rushed them on board the nearest barges. With help from their mates the walking wounded quickly followed. Then the remaining troops charged out through the water to fling themselves onto the nearest barges or into the sea to swim. The beach was cleared in five minutes. Men carried only their weapons as they had been instructed to leave everything else on the beach. Many had booby-trapped their abandoned packs with grenades.

For Private Ned Marsterson of the Mortar Platoon, as for many others, the evacuation experience has remained a traumatic memory. He recalled it in his commentary in *The Savage Shore:*

> 'When they said the barges were going to come in, it was half past two Saturday afternoon, bright sunshine not a cloud in the sky, and you've got to run out into the water and there's machine- guns firing at you – it makes you think. There were wounded who were starting to pile up. Well they got them down first, somebody had to sneak them out.
>
> 'How we never got mowed down in the water by those machine-guns – they were concentrating on the barges coming in and I think that the Japs thought there were reinforcements coming in. They thought "We'll knock them first and get these fellows afterwards". But it wasn't that at all – they were trying to come in and get us out.'

Enemy fire was horrendous during the dash, with fire coming from both flanks as well as from the area which had just been vacated. No further casualties were suffered on the beach as it was being cleared, but many troops were wounded or killed as they fled through the water to the waiting barges. The Corsairs, led by R.A.A.F. Boomerangs, resumed bombing and strafing Japanese gun positions as soon as the men had left the beach.

Those troops who reached the barges first were able to clamber aboard but the vessels quickly became so overcrowded and overloaded that they eventually bottomed-out on the reef. Late-comers were forced to swim from one craft to another looking for any available space on board. Some hardy swimmers chose to take their chances and swim out to the LC15s waiting offshore, or to small islands in Matchin Bay. At all times they were under threat from snipers' bullets, the relentless automatic fire from the shore, and hungry sharks and crocodiles.

Private Merv Porter recalls his retreat to the beach after the rescue barges had grounded:

> 'On the beach I could see one barge already heading out to sea, and another stuck on the coral reef with a dead man hanging in the Vickers MG harness. There was one barge still on the beach and that is where we headed. Coddy beat me by a nose but nobody came after us. We got on board and the barge door was closed and away we went only to be stuck on the beach again – this time side on.
>
> 'The Japs opened up on us and it was like hail on a tin roof. They must have wasted 1000s of rounds.'

The survivors' memories of the hours which followed the withdrawal show clearly that many being rescued were not escaping from the hell on Porton beach, as they thought. Instead, they were taking that hell with them – into a sea infested with sharks and salt-water crocodiles, where their old enemy the coral reef also lay in wait for them; and onto the decrepit and unseaworthy landing barges in which they were placing all their trust and hope. Private Ned Marsterson recalls:

> 'Well, I waded out through the water up to my shoulders and as soon as there was any explosion in the water the sharks were there, and that was the worrying part for me because I'd had a couple of brushes. They had a great time – they didn't care if they ate Australian, Japanese or American.'

Major Dick Sampson who was at TacHQ at this time obtained permission to go to Porton in an LC 15 to assist with the evacuation. He recorded:

> 'During the whole time both ALCAs and LC15s were subjected to heavy SA fire and craft crews suffered severe casualties. Our barge stood in close and picked up 12. We transferred the rescued personnel to a now-empty ALCA which was sinking but was estimated to be capable of reaching base. Our gunner, Private Golding, kept firing continuously and his part of the craft was well splattered with fire, including one shot through his trousers, two through his gun, and one through the Vickers belt causing a stoppage. Our LC15 remained in the area to give cover to the ALCAs which had become stranded on the coral. Manoeuvring the LC15s close in was very difficult

for the coxswains due to the numerous reefs and several times barges ran aground and had to be towed off.'

Captain Stuart Leslie was in charge of the ALCA *Yorkshire Rose.* He recalls the evacuation:

> 'My barge was considerably overloaded and stuck fast. I remember thinking, "what a terrible way to die after all these years in the Army!" I persuaded many of the troops to go back into the water on the side away from the enemy fire. This lightened the load and we floated off the reef. The troops climbed back on board and we moved out to sea. We collected dead and wounded from the LC15s and headed for the forward ("Freddie") Beach. A big problem was caused by water coming in through holes in the barge deck caused by coral. We managed to stop the holes by jamming .303 rounds into them'.

The remaining two ALCAs , overloaded with fleeing personnel and now firmly grounded, became fixed and stationary targets for the full force and fury of Japanese guns and mortars, as well as their artillery from Chabai village 1kilometre away.

The troops who reached the first of the two grounded ALCAs, No.900, braved that torrent of enemy automatic and small arms fire while they made several determined but unsuccessful efforts to push it off the reef. This resulted in many more casualties and the men were forced to return to comparative safety behind of the bullet-proof hull of their barge. Private Merv. Porter and his mate Ron Codrington of 8 Platoon were aboard ALCA 900. Merv recalled the tragedy of those courageous efforts to free the vessel:

> 'Ascertaining that there were ropes on the side of the barge it was decided that four of us would go over the side and pull the barge off the beach, using the craft as cover till we got into deeper water. Jack Salmon was the first to go but unfortunately he got caught in a burst of machine-gun fire, was hit in the head and had to be pulled back into the barge. That left three of us to go and we all went over the side together. All was going well until the driver started the engine, swung the barge around and exposed us to fire from the beach. The other two lads were hit and went down immediately and I copped one across the right shoulder.
>
> 'The wash from the barge propeller pushed the other two further from the barge. They both had their packs on which made them easy targets and they copped more fire. I made my way to the front of the barge which by now was stuck on the beach again. With the Japs firing at me I was yelling all the time for someone to open the door. They did and I got back in the barge in one heave and it was shut behind me. I had a bloke I did not know put a field dressing on my shoulder.'

Following his escape from the beach Lieutenant Blue Reiter also reached ALCA 900 which was carrying many of the wounded. He reported:

> 'When I got onto the barge it was grounded by being overloaded. I told the troops they were free to swim to barges further out and that I was staying with the wounded. While swimming out a number were killed or wounded by heavy Jap fire.

> 'A Private Ward was the only other uninjured man on board and he stayed with me and the wounded. Little "Wardy" had come to me under odd circumstances and wore me like a shadow. When 6 smoke canisters landed on the upper deck he ran past me, jumped on the upper deck and threw them into the sea with his bare hands, all the time under Jap fire. Otherwise if the barge had caught fire we would all have had it. For this he got the D.C.M. signed for by me and the barge crew.'

Lieutenant Keith Scoble and the six other ranks of his A.S.C. unit made their various ways to this barge at about 6.30 p.m. during a slight lull in enemy fire. With the exception of Corporal Tymms they all became casualties. Keith Scoble recalls:

> 'We settled down to what turned out to be a long wait. There was nothing we could do except to keep a watch to ensure we were not surprised by Jap patrols with grenades. One of the wounded died. We decided that those who were able should jump overboard and make a break for the relief barges, thus enabling the barge with the others aboard to get away on the midnight tide. Most of those few who were to make the break discarded all clothing, boots and socks. But a couple of us kept our shirts and slacks on as we were strong swimmers, and in case we were forced to make for the beach and go into the jungle.
>
> 'Eventually we reached an LC15 to our south. Several of the chaps were badly wounded by the Jap as they were swimming and had to be hauled on the barge. When we were out of range

Pte. "Stiffy Flynn "A" Coy. 31/51[s] Infantry Battalion A.I.F Porton June 1945 Bougainville.

of the enemy guns we transferred to another ALCA which pulled alongside. It was rather difficult lifting the wounded men from one barge to the other but we soon had them as comfortable as possible. A couple of men fell overboard and were recovered although nearly drowned.

'We landed at "Freddie" Beach at about 11.00pm on Saturday night. Great regard is held for those engineer and watercraft personnel who went in time and time again to rescue us. The action was an expensive one in men and equipment and, but for these men it would have been considerably more so, particularly in manpower.'

When Private Stiffy Flynn reached the last remaining grounded ALCA, No.213, it was lying parallel to the beach with its door wide open. Unknown to him, it was also holed by coral and stuck hard and fast on the reef. It was destined never to leave Porton. Stiffy recalled that time:

'I dived into it and fell into a foot of water. What a shelter! A rush of troops followed me and in what seemed like seconds the wrecked barge was a mass of bodies, some of them wounded. When the rush subsided we closed the doors. We came under light fire but knew if they brought up any heavy stuff it would be curtains for all of us. We assumed they would wait for daylight to finish us off. Anyone who chanced swimming out to sea did so with the understanding that there was no return once you left the ALCA. This was because you could be mistaken for a Jap and shot as you approached the barge again.'

R.A.A.F "Boomerang"

R.N.Z.A.F "Corsair" Bomber

Saturday, June 9 – Day 2

The Barge 12

Captain Downs and 60 troops, including 12 wounded, were packed into the confined space of this ALCA, No. 213. With a jagged hole in the bottom it was rapidly filling with water and had been judged by the barge crew to be unsalvageable. Enemy fire was now focused on the crippled vessel and its exhausted occupants. For many hours the men crouched low in the water inside the armoured hull while bullets battered the barge.

As they waited to be rescued the troops fended off Japanese attacks but their situation was precarious. Private Wal Crawford, 31st/51st Intelligence Officer, boarded this craft with Captain Downs after the beach was cleared. Detached and dispassionate, he recorded his findings:

> 'The ALCA gunners fired at the enemy along the beach with their Vickers and Brownings until they themselves were killed or the guns rendered unserviceable. Water had reached a level of 30centimetres in our barge, flooding the engine and ruining the wireless set. The flooding and number of personnel on the craft caused suffering to the wounded so Captain Downs ordered everyone to remove their boots to prevent further injury.'

To these men who were now isolated and besieged in the sinking barge their rescue from Porton had become a cruel hoax. For them nothing had changed. Reports of the time showed that they were still trapped and crouching in dirty water under a scorching sun, as they had been for the previous thirty-six hours in their weapon pits. They were still being deafened, wounded and killed by the Japanese unrelenting gunfire as they were on Porton beach; and there was no respite. They were without drinking water and had only the most meagre of rations, as before, and ammunition and medical supplies were still seriously limited. Once again all radio contact had been lost. And again, the only escape was by taking to the sea.

When Captain Blue Shilton boarded this ALCA he found himself thinking of his three-week-old daughter. He was trying to resign himself to this incomprehensible reality, that his life " had come to this – after all the many months of front-line duty!" It had come to this - a badly botched and bloody operation which from the beginning had been pointless and, above all, unnecessary. The good men around him were suffering and dying for nothing and he was starkly reminded that he too might not survive to see his wife again or hold his baby daughter.

From his position on the barge Blue Shilton had a view of the troops who were attempting to push the nearby grounded ALCA 900 off the reef. In *The Savage Shore* he described the horror of the scene:

> 'They tried to push it off soon after they got aboard. They were absolutely massacred, the fellows that got off, and I could see it happening. It was terrible. Men were just dropping off the side of the barge but they weren't able to push it off. They waited then until high tide during the night and they poled it off using rifles and bayonets.'

Wounded during the withdrawal, Blue Shilton knew that his right arm was useless. Nevertheless, after dark when Captain Downs told those who wished to swim to have a go, he decided to take a chance:

> 'I swam in company with others to an LC15 grounded on the reef. Swimming was very difficult using only one arm. I went under several times, swallowed a bit of water and managed to survive the machine-gun fire directed at us. The LC15 was unarmoured and not a very safe spot so we decided to crawl to the bow and the heavy ramp which offered greater protection from the machine-gun fire. Later an ALCA took us off, then down to "Freddie" Beach and the Advanced Dressing Staion.
>
> 'I got the greatest fit of the shivers ever on the way back, just could not control it. Maybe the stress of the previous thirty-six hours had something to do with it. The Advanced Dressing Station orderlies washed us, dressed our wounds, gave us pyjamas, a meal and a stretcher - slept like a log. Many wounded came in during the next few hours and the doctors were still operating hours later.'

Private Fred Stamp, with five chest wounds, was taken to the rescue barges and then on to the Advanced Dressing Station at "Freddie" Beach. Later when his mates Fred Horlock and Harry Brodie went there to find him Fred was missing from his bed. There was pandemonium for a time but he was located eventually in the shower – despite the five wounds in his chest! When they asked what it was like at Porton he replied, "Hell and mighty bloody dangerous!"

Viv Taylor of the 19 Field Ambulance was another of the unfortunate occupants of ALCA 213. Following the confusion which ensued after first boarding the craft he found himself up to his neck in water:

> 'I have very vivid memory of the Vickers gunner on the barge blasting away from a pretty exposed position and being cut down by a woodpecker burst from the beach. He was dead before he hit the deck – another brave young Aussie lost to us all. I can still hear the Japs' yells of jubilation as they went through our bags left behind on the beach. I know I had two quarter-pound blocks of chocolate in mine. I recall sitting in the barge defenceless, a sitting duck.
>
> 'The Japs threw everything at us. The barge Vickers gun was not manned – two gunners had been killed in quick succession. The Skipper asked if anyone would like to man it but there was no response. The water in the barge was heavy with battery acid and blood from the dead and wounded. After dark the Japs sent out boats and sprayed the barge with machine-gun fire. Captain Downs was by now badly wounded with what looked to me like little hope of survival, but he still had the courage and compassion to give the order, "Every man for himself!" It was shortly after 1.00 a.m., when the Japs came aboard and sprayed us with fire, that I and others climbed out of the barge to swim.'

While enemy automatic fire continued unabated, mortar shells began to fall near the vessel and difficulties on board multiplied. The overcrowding, with the wounded lying on the floor and the water steadily rising, meant that all movement was severely restricted. Captain Downs had received a shrapnel wound to his face and jaw, and was now bleeding profusely from the mouth.

These problems were further compounded by the coming of darkness and the high tide. The seriously wounded had to be held above water. The danger of a mortar shell falling into this confined space was obvious and Captain Downs urged the able-bodied troops to swim to the LC15s waiting out at sea, or to one of the smaller islands in Matchin Bay. Finally, at around midnight when he announced "Every man for himself!" sixteen men took to the water. For the remainder, crowded in their dark, flooded prison, there was no comfort to be had, not even a cigarette or a drink of water. In the midst of this nightmare their chief objective was to keep their heads above the rising tide, and stay alive. Hopes of survival were being severely tested.

An attempt to rescue the stranded troops was made late that night by Major Sampson and Captain Leslie. Leslie and his crew in an ALCA, the *Yorkshire Rose*, went in two or three times despite intense Japanese fire and succeeded in picking up 40 to 50 men, many from the stores barge which had now been evacuated. Captain Leslie reported:

> 'We came back at night to try and pick up survivors but the landing craft were in very poor mechanical condition. I was using the only serviceable craft that night and we managed to save quite a number of troops. I saw a hand in the water and when I leaned over to grab it the hand turned out to be Captain Shilton M.C. We have been friends ever since.'

Major Sampson in an LC15 recorded his part in the rescue:

> 'Our LC15 [was to] go in to the stranded stores barge and bring off any troops who might happen to be on it. Our barge was unable to get right in

to the stores barge owing to the reef, but when in close, I became aware of a man struggling in the water. When we got near him, I went overboard and brought him to the craft. It was Private de Burgh [off the stores barge] who was able to assure us that there was no-one left on that craft. Because of engine trouble Captain Leslie decided to return to base with the ALCA, have the matter attended to and come back later in the night.

'In the LC15 we drew considerable fire whenever we came in close. I was anxious to get accurate information about the numbers left on the stranded ALCAs 900 and 213, so a Water Transport Private and I attempted swimming in on a kapok raft with a few lifejackets attached, but a strong southerly current prevented us from making it. By this time the LC15 was very short of fuel and we returned to "I" Beach.'

A personal account of this, the first, rescue which also shows the growing desperation of the survivors in the wrecked ALCA 213, appears in the unpublished memoirs of Alan Graham, the Browning gunner on the *Yorkshire Rose:*

'Our Captain [Leslie] came aboard from a fifty-four footer [LC 15] that was cruising off the beach. There were six aboard the Yorkshire Rose when we commenced the run in. The crew of three and the Captain, the Vickers gunner, and Nugget from the workshops who explained his presence by saying, "I believe some of the motors seized under pressure."

'The coxswain, Percy, headed for the sunken barge. I could see the blue pinpoints of fire from many points directly in front.

'"Open up," ordered the Captain.

'"I will as soon as I can line something up. There is no point in firing wild."

'Then I cranked up the heavy machine gun and let it go.

' Percy nosed the Rose up to the stern of the sunken barge and I could no longer fire so decided to help otherwise.

'"Wounded first," ordered the Captain.

'I heard pleas for help coming from under the barge door and the stern of the sunken one. Not taking any chances in case of Jap trickery I took my rifle with me to lean over the door to see three Diggers waiting there in waist deep water.

'"Give us a hand mate," one said.

'I reached over with my right hand and it was grabbed by three pairs of hands.

'"Let go, I cannot pull three of you aboard at once."

'Reluctantly two finally released my arm and I could not even pull one aboard because of the backward slope of the door.

'"Let go. I cannot pull you in. You will have to go around the side where I can stand on the catwalk and hoist you up."

'"How do we know that you will do what you say?" said the spokesman.

'"We can drag you in with us," said another.

'"Don't be an idiot. If I go in, no-one gets out."

'"Promise you won't leave us."

'"I promise," I replied and my hand was released.

'I stood on the catwalk and dragged aboard one after the other.

'"Get down off there," roared Percy, "or you will get your head knocked off."

'I jumped to the deck and saw by the feeble light coming through the small engine room door Nugget trying to haul Jimmy out of the engine room and I went to his assistance. The engine room was full of fumes and running water could be heard. It was quickly deduced that Jimmy had succumbed to the fumes and Nugget took his place. I dragged Jimmy up forward where I did my best to render artificial respiration.

'Percy reversed the barge.

'The Captain said, "We will unload the men aboard and return."

'One man only heard the second part of the statement and said, "You are not bloody well going to take us back in THERE!"

'We tied up to a fifty- four footer and transferred the men'

When reporting on this successful rescue bid Major Dick Sampson was critical of Artillery's lack of ammunition:

> 'At this stage no artillery was available to give support owing to lack of ammunition and I am certain that had it been available we would have got all troops off [the barges] that night.'

Shortly after midnight Private Joe Patterson and a small group swam from the sunken ALCA 213 to the deserted stores barge which lay about 200 metres away on the reef. Captain Downs had instructed them to investigate the possibility of moving some of the troops onto this craft, and retrieving the ammunition and rations on board. However these hopes were dashed when a hostile native on the stores barge confronted the group and forced them to withdraw. Hardly had they done so when the stores barge suddenly burst into flames. At almost the same moment a phosphorous grenade was lobbed in the stern of ALCA 213 and the whole scene lit up brilliantly. Taking advantage of the illumination the Japanese redoubled their attack and swept the ALCA with concentrated machine-gun fire.

The Intelligence Report by Private Crawford on ALCA 213 stated:

> 'Those in the centre of the barge were swept by fire and in a surge forward to escape the fire several were swept overboard, taking Captain Downs with them.'

Crawford recalled that the C.O. grasped his forehead as he toppled over the side and he believes Captain Downs had received another gunshot wound to the head. He was not seen again. At the time it was thought that the C.O. had been shot and swept out to sea, or taken by a shark. A thorough aerial reconnaissance later sighted a body fitting his description floating face-down in the bay but a positive identification was not possible. Some of the troops managed to return to the barge and some were later picked up on the outer reef by patrolling barges. Sharks were seen.

According to Private Crawford's report, by 3.00 a.m. the fire in the stores barge had been reduced and there was also a lull in the firing. The Japanese then made several determined efforts to swim out in the darkness to throw grenades into the ALCA. Always watchful, the men on board who still had guns were able to pick them off as they approached because phosphorescence in the water revealed their position. The Japanese trick of calling out in English, for example, "I am Johnson, I am blind, come and help me", did not succeed. Loud screaming in Japanese which followed one such attempt seemed to indicate the speaker had been taken by a shark.

After 5.00 a.m. all was quiet for a time. TacR aircraft circling overhead kept the enemy guns silent. At first light the men in the ALCA saw the waiting LC15 rescue barges offshore, out of range of the enemy guns. In the absence of wireless communication the men used an electric light bulb and a battery to attract the attention of their rescuers. The troops needed to let them know there were still live men on board their beleaguered craft. There was no response. The circling TacR pilot reported that he had seen no movement inside the stranded ALCA.

During the lull the survivors on board checked their situation and supplies in an effort to reorganize themselves while they waited for the rescuers they never doubted would come. There were 38 men alive and 2 dead. Lists were drawn up.

<u>Weapons:</u> 2 Bren light machine guns, 5 Owens, 9 Rifles

<u>Ammunition:</u> 12 Bren magazines with a good supply of .303 ammunition, small supply 9mm.

<u>Rations:</u> 2 tins tomato juice, 1 tin tomatoes, 3 tins carrot juice, 1 tin cabbage, 3 tins condensed milk, 2 tins pears, ¾ tin corned beef.

Medical: 1 large first aid outfit, with morphia and shell dressings. Several individual field dressings.

Drinking water: Nil.

After the loss of Captain Downs it was necessary that a substitute leader be appointed for the barge as quickly as possible. Sergeant Boon of 19 Field Ambulance had the highest rank on board but he declined command in favour of an infantryman, Corporal Eric Hall of "A" Company, who was chosen by the troops and was the next most senior in rank.

Corporal Eric Hall "A" Coy 31st/51^{s} Inf. Bn.

Eric Hall was a twenty-three-year-old bank clerk from north Queensland who was well used to meeting the challenges on local sporting fields. He proved more than equal to this challenge. Demonstrating natural organizational skills, sound judgment and leadership in this difficult and dangerous situation, Eric was to become a legend at Porton. In a very practical way he helped to support and direct the shattered men in his care until the last rescue barges came for them, almost 30 hours later.

Hall quickly drew up a defensive plan of action. This included removing the existing wooden shelves and placing them overhead, thus providing more space and also protection from small arms fire; throwing the ruined wireless set overboard to make extra space; issuing each man with a 15 centimetre length of copper pipe (salvaged by an engineer from the disabled engine) to be used as a snorkel when the water rose in the barge with the incoming tide. Hall ordered a watch to be kept at all times to report on enemy movements.

Private Crawford's report gave more details of the action plan:

> 'Weapons were cleaned and oiled with a lubricant taken from the engines and issued to personnel capable of cleaning the weapons. The Medical kit was given to Sergeant Boon, the medical orderly with the Field Ambulance detachment. He issued the morphia and dressings as required. The rations were retained by Corporal Hall and issued only with his permission. The limited fluids [liquid from tins of fruit and vegetables] were to be reserved for the wounded.'

Noting that everyone in the barge was suffering from exposure, lack of food, water and sleep Hall immediately commenced rationing out the available stores. In the midst of tragedy he was able to restore a sense of order and purpose.

One of the wounded on the ALCA was Tony Moyse of the 11th Brigade Signals Section. The compassionate treatment he received at that time from Eric Hall, who installed him in a corner away from the flying shrapnel, has remained one of his treasured memories. He first became a casualty while waiting on the beach to be evacuated:

> 'I felt a sensation like an electric shock on my left thigh and realized I had been shot. The bullet

had gone right through to the other side of my leg. I hobbled out to a barge which unfortunately was unable to move.

'I did not know the name of the man who took control of those on board the barge but I am sure that I survived because of his efforts. Many years later I read a report on the Porton campaign which mentioned Corporal Hall and I was able to get in touch with him to thank him. I had lost everything except the clothes I was wearing and I just had to wait until rescued, or otherwise, while things were happening around us. I never lost hope and always felt that I would survive.'

With obvious emotion Lance Corporal Joe Chapel, 2 Platoon 16 Field Company (R.A.E.) and section "medic", told of his hours on the doomed ALCA as the tide rose and the wounded lay helpless in the bottom of the barge. The man beside him was dying and Joe held him in his arms, out of the water, until he passed away. Joe himself had been wounded in the hip and a metal object was still painfully embedded there.

As he belonged to the Engineers Joe set himself the task of fashioning snorkels out of copper piping from the barge's wrecked engine. These gave the men, especially the wounded on the floor of the barge, the opportunity to breathe more confidently once the craft began to flood with the incoming tide. One of the wounded was Private Bill Aspinall . With shrapnel in his knee and a wounded hand he was unfit to swim from the barge to safety. He was grateful for Joe's "bright idea – it worked!"

Eventually deciding to take his chances in the sea despite his injury, Joe Chapel left the barge and swam to an LC15 which waited offshore out of range of the enemy's guns. It was there that he was later able to give First Aid to his commanding officer Lieutenant Arthur Graham who had arrived on board after being wounded by friendly fire during a rescue attempt with assault boats.

Felix Grasso

The late Felix Grasso's chilling testimony in *The Savage Shore* described the endurance of the men incarcerated on the ill-fated ALCA 213:

'Being in that barge was like being in a bloody coffin. When you've got space around you, you can do something about it but when you're in a confined space with wounded blokes you have to look after, it was pretty grim. There were badly wounded fellas there and we had them in our arms. We had to take them with us, the moment we let them go they sank in the water so we just couldn't move.

'No way in the world would we have surrendered – one bloke wanted to but we wouldn't let him – no way in the world. We knew what our fate would be, we watched them bayonet the wounded on the beach and couldn't do anything about it. We could see them on the shore robbing our dead and they were wearing our uniforms and souveniring anything they could find. We were watching them but there was nothing we could do about it.

'But we never gave up hope.

'Never!'

Sunday, June 10 – Day 3

Rescue 13

Major Sampson knew that it was imperative to retrieve the troops still trapped on the two stranded ALCAs, 213 and 900, without delay. He knew that their situation would now be desperate. He drew up a plan to use an LC15 and assault boats for a rescue during the night of Sunday, June 10.

Barges at "Freddie Beach" Bougainville 9 June 1945.

However, in the meantime, ALCA 900 with Lieutenant Blue Reiter and the wounded men aboard had managed to float off the reef on the high tide, seven hours after the evacuation. When they arrived back at "Freddie" Beach at midnight Blue immediately requested another barge to take him back to Porton in a bid to rescue the troops on the remaining ALCA 213. This was refused by the Landing Craft officer who stated that his men had had no sleep for thirty-six hours and they would not be able to guarantee the safety of the craft. Blue's reply was characteristically blunt:

> 'My reply was that neither had I or the men in the stranded barge and we had been in action all the time. After four hours at Brigade HQ I finally got a barge and went back. By this time daylight was breaking and the stores barge was still burning. So the Japs, after seeing us, we were heavily engaged and could not get close. Picked up 8 men swimming. I still maintain to this day that had a barge been immediately given we may have rescued a lot more. I have never forgiven those of Brigade for it.'

In a concerted effort to rescue the last survivors on ALCA 213, Major Sampson had requested an airstrike at dusk to drive the enemy out of their positions. He also asked for assault boats to be sent up to Porton as soon as possible and the Brigade Major stated that this would be done. An LC15 was the only barge available for the rescue attempt. Although it was obvious that the unarmoured LC15 would have little chance of reaching shore in daylight in the face of intense enemy fire, the airstrike took place at mid-afternoon instead of at dusk. Sampson reported:

> 'The airstrike took place at 3.30 p.m. and artillery brought down fire. The airstrike was a success and eliminated all but small arms fire until after the final rescue. Rubber rafts were dropped [by Beaufort and Mitchell bombers] but these overshot the craft and we picked them up later. In an LC15 we got within 50 metres of the ALCA after the strike but were met by heavy small arms fire. One soldier tried to swim out and was shot.'

An assault boat was launched crewed by 16 Field Company Sappers Jim Hackett and Alf Hartley. They trailed a line from the LC15 for the rescue but this fouled on the reef and had to be discarded. When the coxswain of the LC15 was wounded and the craft's rudder cable almost severed the attempt had to be abandoned. Major Sampson continued:

> 'We moved away from the shore and I reported to Brigade by wireless and was ordered to return [to base]. We replied "able to continue" but as the order was repeated we complied. This was a mistake because had we remained in the area we would have prevented the Japanese from closing with the stranded barge'.

Sampson's rescue plan which had seemed so promising had failed. For the weary and dispirited troops on ALCA 213 there stretched ahead a second horrific night of Japanese mortar and gunfire and treacherous grenade attacks. Eric Hall was alarmed to see that the enemy had mounted a juki on the burnt-out stores barge so that they had the ALCA in crossfire at point-blank range. He reported,

> 'The Japs are also attempting to observe our numbers from a tree. We keep out of sight on the floor of the barge where the water is up to our waists.'

Private Crawford described the pitiful condition of the men around him in the barge:

> 'The intense heat and the exposure and the fact that we had not slept for three days and nights were beginning to take effect. Men collapsed due to exhaustion and a few were delirious. Men

were suffering from deafness caused by exploding bombs, shells and small arms fire - and from thirst.'

The worst fears of the stranded troops were confirmed on the night of June 10. Private Crawford's report continued:

'At about 1.00 a.m. a lone Japanese clambered on the stern of the craft, momentarily catching everyone off guard, and sprayed the occupants with a light machine-gun. He was killed, but not before he killed two and wounded several others. Immediately he was killed, the Japs opened fire from the jetty with tracer and explosive bullets that wounded still more. After 18 minutes of heavy machine-gun fire, a Tank-Attack gun fired two rounds at the ALCA tearing the stern from the craft.' It flooded immediately.

Gavin Long's official report in "The Final Campaigns" describes the action on the barge directly following that attack:

'Immediately the Australian artillery opened fire and the Japanese fire ceased. This artillery fire raised the spirits of the weary men on the barge, especially when a shell landed among a group of Japanese who were swimming out towards them. In the event of rescue Hall had given orders that the wounded were to go first, then the Owen gunners [who were short of ammunition], then the riflemen and finally the Bren gunners.'

Two of the men wounded by the suicide gunner had been sitting close to Eric Hall. He recalls,

> 'Jim Pitcher on my right got a bullet in the arm and the man next to him one in the stomach. They both called my name and as I turned my head a bullet struck the metal protection I was firing around and sprayed me down the left side of my head. Had they not called my name and I turned my head, I most probably would be blinded. At that time I was endeavouring to take the waterproofing off a bandage with my teeth to cover Jim's arm wound.
>
> 'At this stage there were only about seven of us on our feet and very tired. We could hear a boat coming. The Arty opened up and put the juki out of commission and also pasted the shore juki which had us in crossfire.'

Meanwhile Major Sampson, following his failed rescue effort, had reluctantly returned to base convinced that had they remained longer in the area with the LC15 they could have prevented the Japanese gunner from boarding the stranded barge and causing more casualties. After a conference at "I" beach Brigade finally agreed to the use of the assault boats once more in another rescue attempt.

In his history of 31st/51st Infantry Battalion Major W. Hughes describes these flimsy craft:

> 'These assault boats, as well as the ALCAs, came from *HMS Glory*. They had plywood bottoms with wooden cleats as runners. The sides were of painted canvas, held up with struts knocked into brass sockets. They were built for river crossings in Europe and were not the most comfortable conveyance to trust against a determined enemy.'

AWM067693. Flimsy canvas assault boats like these, designed for river crossings, were paddled in from an LC15, waiting out at sea, to rescue the last of the survivors on the stranded A.L.C.A.

Lieut. Arthur Graham M.C.
C.O. 2 Platoon 16 FD. Coy.
(R.A.E.) Porton June 1945.
Bougainville

For Major Sampson's rescue bid two LC15s were sent to Porton together with three assault boats. Lieutenant Arthur Graham 16 Field Company, with eight engineers, came to operate the assault boats. Lieutenant Graham described the preparation for the rescue and gave an account of the action from his perspective as commander of 2 Platoon 16 Field Company:

'Despite air-support, stealthy night-time attempts at rescue from the sea, and air-drops of floatation gear, this flat, ill-shapen hell of Porton was bracketed by withering enemy fire, frustrating all sea-borne rescue attempts.

'Out of the anger, sorrow and almost despair of the moment, a meeting was arranged to stage what appeared to be a last-ditch attempt. The array of talent included local Commanders and extra support from 11 Brigade Headquarters. From one of these came an astounding suggestion that an ALCA should by night approach the stranded barge and from this small, wind-swept base a kapok Assault Bridge would be launched! This European-designed structure was intended for crossing small, still-water streams, and to be launched from a fixed terra-firma base. Its launching was controlled by guy-ropes operated from the riverbank while it was projected bay by bay. A cross-river cable secured the alignment, using rope slings. It was obvious to the majority that none of these elements of stability and control could be afforded by a sea-borne craft. [Indeed, the volume of the gear involved would have been too great for the capacity of the landing barge.]

'Which left us with another river-designed facility – the "ASSAULT" boat - boasting a cleated plywood bottom and painted canvas, strut-supported sides [even in training on Lake Somerset we'd been troubled by its turbulence.] The final decision was that the LC15 would move in as far as prudently possible and then launch the assault boats. This, at least, was a possible procedure. They would be crewed by the sappers, by that time much used to picking-up-the-pieces. However, in this case, apart from being a duty which was never shirked, there was a strong personal incentive. We believed that Corporal Bertram's sapper section was a participant in this sorry saga and sheer mateship made it more than being just to take on any challenge which might arise.

'So Graham, Draper and Dosetto led off in Boat No. 1. I wore only a jungle green shirt – holding a .3 S&W in my right hand and a grenade in the left. The burning question was – where was this stranded craft? We were not even sure of the position of our starting LC15. At about 2.00 a.m. on 11 June 1945 it was mercifully dark. We were trailing a light contact cord as a link to the LC15 but it soon fouled on the reef and was cast off. The Arty had scraped together enough 25 pounder ammo to pound the shore-line in advance of our approach. This caused much smoke and dust which severely restricted visibility. One projectile whistled close in, to strike the sea about the length of a cricket pitch ahead. It did not detonate.

'So we probed about, at one stage hearing excited Japanese chatter not far ahead. Frantic but fairly silent back-paddling ensued. In addition, the phosphorescence caused by paddling was surprisingly bright in the warm, near-equatorial waters and was of some concern. After much careful navigation on my part, and sturdy seamanship on the part of the redoubtable Draper and Dosetto, we made out a shadowy shape and proceeded to move alongside. Almost there, we were met with a burst of Owen-gun fire – 8-10 rounds.'

Eric Hall took up the story:

> 'We challenged the boat coming because it appeared to be coming from behind the stores barge and we thought them to be Japs. When they didn't answer our challenge, and being in the state we were in, we took them for Japs and opened fire, wounding the Lieutenant in charge. They called out then and were recognised. Rescue was effected, 5 and 7 in the first two boats – the worst of the wounded went first.
>
> 'When the boats returned, the balance of the numbers were loaded, 12 in one boat and 14 in the other. Myself and a Water Transport member checked the barge out, disposed of weapons left behind and joined the row boats. There were 38 rescued, wounded and able, and I would say they were 38 very lucky men. Our rescue would have been effected by 5.30 a.m. on Monday 11 June 1945.'

The small assault boats were perilously overloaded. According to Major Sampson, the engineers knew that time was running short and they bravely "took the risk of sinking the assault craft by bringing them out with only 5 – 7 centimetres of freeboard, swimming and pushing the boats themselves."'

Sampson's account of the rescue confirmed Lieutenant Graham's report. He added:

> 'When Lieutenant Graham led his Engineers in the assault boats each man wore a life jacket and there were 26 carried in the boats for the troops on the ALCA.

'Boat 1 carried Lt. Graham, Cpl. Draper, Spr. Dosetto (later replaced by Sgts. Blondell and Jack);

'Boat 2: Sprs. Halford and Deller;

'Boat 3: Sprs. Owen and Coulsen.

'After a long period Graham's boat returned with 5 rescued soldiers. Unfortunately he was mistaken for the enemy and troops on the ALCA fired two machine gun bursts into his boat. He was wounded in the stomach, arm and shoulder and Corporal Draper was also wounded. They were returned to "I" beach and the other Engineers returned to the rescue. One boat was holed and the other might be any time. The Engineers were not inexhaustible and the men on ALCA 213 were too weak to help themselves with the life jackets.

'Water Transport had told me that an ALCA would be ready later in the night. I decided to get it.

'Signals:

"If ALCA is repaired send it up".

"ALCA serviceable STOP no guns no ammunition is it still required".

"Yes we want ALCA and quick. If ALCA not already left send medical orderly and estimated time of arrival".

'Intercepted by the radio operator on my LC15 "Brigade Major has cancelled sailing of ALCA".

'We sent – "imperative we have ALCA STOP there is no risk we are getting them off".

"ALCA is not available will not be sent".

'Our last message was possibly unfortunately worded but those in rear were only making guesses at the situation and requests from those on the spot should have been granted. By sheer good luck we rescued the remainder but the results had every chance of being different. Interference from rear came again with a signal for the barge with 12 rescued men to return. This was ill-advised as it is most dangerous to have a craft on its own amongst the reefs at night. The 12 were actually the best-conditioned of those rescued; there was no harm in keeping the other LC15 and every reason to do so.

'The two assault boats returned. Blondell and Jack had rescued 12 and Owen and Coulson 11. They knew that artillery ammunition was short so took the risk of sinking the assault craft by bringing off the remainder. Blondell did a thorough search of the ALCA before leaving and is certain that only the dead remained. It was not possible to take them off or any of the weapons. These later he dismantled and threw into the sea.

'We then set to work to get rescued over the side. Except two, all had to be lifted. The pain the burned and wounded suffered was heartbreaking. The rescue party gave their clothes to those suffering from shock and exhaustion. At about 3.00 a.m. we made full speed back to "F" Beach where all rescued were admitted to the Medical Dressing Station. I went to "I" Beach and went to bed.'

For 35 hours the men on ALCA 213 had visited the very heart of darkness. And the survivors remember it well.

The force had fought a continuous action against a numerically superior enemy, both in manpower and weapons, on land, for 35 hours 25 minutes. The withdrawal took 35 hours 30 minutes to complete. Out of the 10 officers and 180 other ranks comprising the Porton landing force, 8 officers and 168 other ranks had been accounted for, including 4 dead and 101 wounded. Missing amounted to 2 officers and 12 other ranks. The enemy was successful in retaining this area but did so at a heavy cost.

The rescue of the men from the barges was now completed. Only the survivors still swimming in the sea or stranded on the outer reef or islands remained to be saved, and there were many of them.

Porton the battle was over. Porton the story had yet to be told.

The Swimmers 14

After the evacuation many of the troops, some wounded, had taken to the sea, swimming for their lives away from the fatal shore or the grounded and sinking barges. For them the pain and the terror were not yet over. Some reached the outer reef or islands in spite of the presence of sharks and crocodiles and snipers' bullets. Once there, naked and exposed to the blistering tropical sun for many hours without food or water, they could only wait and hope desperately that a patrolling barge would see them and pick them up while they were still alive.

Some who took to the water died there from their wounds or shark or crocodile attacks. Others died from sheer exhaustion. Searching aircraft saw small parties of men on the reef and coastline between Ratsua and Buoi Plantation and off Torokori Island. They were subsequently rescued by assault boats from Ratsua. Patrolling barges picked up survivors in enemy territory for a couple of days after the evacuation. The courage and endurance of these men in the sea almost defies description.

Captain Leslie recalled Sapper Balhorn's impressive swim. After the evacuation he swam back to base at Saposa Is. 'at least 8 kilometres in dangerous waters and visited various islands on the way.'

Corporal Ben Bertram, 16 Field Company (R.A.E.), with Lieutenant Arthur Graham's watch and compass in his pocket, swam three kilometres from the ill-fated ALCA 213, jettisoned the watch and compass because they became too heavy, and then swam another three kilometres before he reached an island. Lieutenant Graham continued Ben's story:

> 'Ben stumbled over coral, cutting his bare feet, and spent the remainder of the night being unwilling host to millions of malicious mossies. Later that morning he attracted the attention of a patrolling ALCA – possibly the only serviceable one left – which was occupied by Gen. Blamey and party. He was welcomed aboard by the coxswain.'

Gunner Deena McHugh recalls in *The Savage Shore:*

> 'One of my gunners was Ron (Peggy) O'Neill. Peggy was from Bowen. And when we got word that we were going to make this landing Peggy said, "If you see a couple of fellas swim over to the island shoot the second bastard, I'll be the one in the lead" and as sure as anything Peggy swam over to the island.'

Signaller Bill Hughes had been on ALCA 213 when Captain Downs advised that those who wished to leave and make their way back to Ratsua should do so. Bill decided to take a chance:

> 'I was a good swimmer. I was joined by Alf Pearce, Ron O'Neill, and the others were a Gunner E.W.Glare, a member of the Mortar Platoon named Bourne, and Lieutenant Joe Patterson. In the dark we made our way to the supply barge where we located two lifebuoys and threw them into the sea. There was a strong smell of petrol, someone saw movement on board, and so we left in great haste. After recovering the life-buoys we headed into the open sea, not knowing where we were going, but

hoping that the tide would deliver us into friendly hands, and the sharks would not molest us. It was now revealed that Joe Patterson and two others could not swim.

'Holding on to the lifebuoys in the darkness we could not orient ourselves and moved with the tide. Fortunately this took us in a southerly direction. We had not gone far when there was a loud explosion and the stores barge burst into flames. The enemy periodically directed his fire at us until we were well out at sea. The swimmers soon started to tire probably because they had not slept for several days and due to the stress of the past few days. We encouraged each other to keep going. Everybody had a fear of sharks.

'About 6.30 a.m. we came to shallow water and walked ashore on to a small island. Everyone was exhausted and moved into the shoreline vegetation and tried to sleep. Soon after we were challenged by someone with an Owen gun. After identifying ourselves we were elated to find we were on Torokori Island and that it was an Observation Post for 4 Field Regiment at Soraken Plantation.

'We were given bread and golden syrup to eat while waiting for breakfast and afterwards an ALCA arrived and delivered us to "I" Beach where we were admitted to the Field Hospital. Our feet were badly lacerated from the jagged coral and black spines from sea urchins were embedded in the soles. I had a large gash on my head and another in my shin and several stitches were inserted in both wounds. A soldier in the bed beside me saw the fiasco at Porton so he and his

> mate decided to return to Ratsua on their own. He was shot just before dark. His mate placed him on a log and dragged him in the sea during the night. Before dawn they hid in the mangroves and when darkness came again they continued on their way in the sea. They were found by a beach patrol and brought to the Field Hospital.'

Stiffy Flynn was also one of the troops who left ALCA 213 to swim to safety, on the understanding that there was no return to the barge:

> 'It was about 2.00 am when a Corporal I knew and another unidentified person opted to swim. As I had no gun and so could not contribute to the defence of our combined group I decided to join them. The Corporal went first and, with 10 metre intervals in between, the other chap next, and then I followed. The second chap was half-way across the lit-up area [the supply barge was on fire] when he gave a muffled scream and disappeared in a large swirl of water. It meant only one thing – a shark attack! I couldn't go back so I went on swimming, trying all the time to avoid the fatal area.
>
> 'Then I found myself alone as the Corporal had also disappeared in the dark. I paddled along quietly hoping to reach Taiof Island about 16 kilometres out, or get picked up by a rescue craft. After about three hours I came across another party of three men and I swam along with them. Two hours later, just on daybreak, a landing barge loomed out of the mist and plucked our little party out of the sea. I turned twenty-two two days later.'

Another man in the sea who endured a long and terrifying swim and survived to tell his remarkable tale of courage was Viv Taylor. Separated from his mate Welshie in the evacuation, he had then sought refuge in ALCA 213. When Captain Downs urged the able-bodied men to swim to safety he had gone overboard with others to swim back to Ratsua. He recalled his experience with some emotion:

> 'I had been talking to Jack Stratford, a 19th Field Ambulance fellow, and a couple of others and we made a decision to swim to Ratsua about 8 kilometres south where we had a base camp of 19th Field Ambulance blokes with a few infantry and engineers. By doing so we thought of giving ourselves a chance of survival and also to be able to notify those back at base of the terrible plight of the fellows stranded on the barge.
>
> 'There was a moon and to give myself maximum chance of surviving the swim I took off all my clothes but made sure my meat ticket was secure around my neck so that if anything went wrong and my body was found they would be able to identify me. When I was ready to leave I looked for the other boys who were going to swim with me but I was unable to find them so I swam off on my own.
>
> 'I didn't really swim but dog-paddled with my body and head as low in the water as possible so I wouldn't be seen from shore. As I moved slowly south there was a headland and I realized when I heard Japs talking that the current was carrying me onto the beach just south of their pill-boxes. So I went quietly further out to sea and headed south and took great care to avoid them seeing me,

swimming as much as possible under water.

'I swam in this way, and well out to sea, for what seemed an eternity until I thought I was well away from the Porton Japs. Then I moved in closer to the shore and was pleased when my feet hit bottom because maybe I could have a rest. However, I soon got a rude awakening because, being on the reef which runs down the west coast of Bougainville, my feet kept standing on spikes which seemed to break off in my feet and the pain was excruciating.

'My first thoughts were that these spikes would poison me and I was alert to any aches and pains through my body. After a time it seemed I would be O.K. but I was very reluctant to touch bottom too often because every time I touched the reef the same painful spikes were there. I later found out that it was sea-urchins that I was standing on and when I got back to hospital at base they set about pulling the spikes out of my feet.

'Swimming on through the night seemed never ending with the fear of shark or crocodile attack ever in mind, the fear of being spotted by the Japs on shore, not knowing if you are in friendly or enemy territory, and the ever-present pain of the sea-urchin spines in the feet. As time went on the hope and determination for survival became stronger and I was almost at peace with myself when I saw in the moonlight a large, dark thing getting close to me. I first thought it was a log but when it was a few feet from me the terrible realization hit me that it was a big crocodile.

'I was terrified and my instinct was to frighten it off [regardless that there may be Japs on shore] by yelling and flaying at it with all my strength and I actually hit the brute with my hand as it glided past. It appeared that he got as big a fright as me because he veered off quickly and appeared to speed faster. Not that I trusted him to keep going. I headed for shore so quick that I may have given a repeat performance of our dear Lord Jesus who walked across the water, but walking was not good enough for me, I ran.

'Close to the shore I picked the biggest tree, a spindly-looking mangrove type, and climbed it as fast as any goanna could. [Not a pleasant experience wearing nothing but your dead- meat ticket], and stayed there until daylight in case that crocodile was hanging around waiting for me to come down, because even if it was Jap territory it seemed better to be dealt with by them than a crocodile.

'Sitting up in the tree as day dawned, I could see no sign of the crocodile but to this day I don't know whether I was hearing things or not. I was sure I could hear bloody Jap voices inland. So I was down off the tree as fast and as quickly as possible and back out to sea, once again headed south, but as it was daylight now I went well out to sea with as little exposure as possible. An hour or so later I heard voices (or thought I did) and gave a couple of loud "Coo-ees" thinking if it was Aussies they would understand, but if it was Japs they wouldn't wake up to what it was. It's marvellous how the mind works in these desperate situations.

‘There was no response to my “Coo-ee” so the voices could not have been Aussies and the only other people around were Japs, and that meant it was necessary to be as little visible as possible. As the morning turned to day and the sun got hotter I realized I was very thirsty and was tempted to drink salt water, but resisted. Then there was a break in the mangroves and what was obviously the mouth of a creek and, if it was running, maybe fresh water.

‘With great care I swam to the mouth of the creek and drank the water. It was still a little salty but was beautiful. An hour or so later I came to a large bay or inlet which I should have realized was the entrance to the area where our base camp was. My mind I think was starting to play tricks and I did some silly things like swimming to shore to have a look and, coming across a bitumen road, walked up and down it a bit not knowing which way to go. Thank God common sense prevailed and I headed back to sea.

‘Then I was standing on a sand bar in the middle of the bay in water about up to my shoulders and I believe the fight for survival was nearing an end and my thinking was getting very negative. It seemed nothing mattered any more. Throughout the day I could hear the New Zealand bombers laying their eggs on Porton, now a few kilometres away. I couldn’t make a decision on what to do next when suddenly two Boomerang fighters came over heading for Porton. Waving my arms frantically and jumping up and down in the water I tried to make them see me. They flew on a little and then one Boomerang turned back and I thought, my God, I hope he doesn't think I am a Jap and turn his guns on me. But he flew low over me and must have been satisfied all was O.K. and dipped his wings and flew off – my hopes were sky high.

'After what seemed like an eternity, and once again the negative thinking returned and I was floundering around like a stunned mullet, there suddenly appeared three blokes rowing a boat. One spoke and it was the sweetest sound I ever heard because it was an Aussie voice. They picked me out of the water and covered me with a blanket. I had spent fourteen hours in the sea. Then one fellow held out a container of water to me and I tried to take it off him but he allowed me only a few sips. I tried to talk to them but they hushed me and said we were still in Jap territory and they were very cautious and prepared for an attack.

'As we moved away they asked if I had been ashore and when I said "yes", and had walked along the road, they were amazed I didn't get blown to Kingdom Come because they said it was a Jap road and they had it heavily mined. So surely someone "up there" was looking after me. The boys who picked me up were from 11th Brigade Engineers and I hope they all survived and lived a long happy life. Thankyou very much. They delivered me to my own 19th Field Ambulance R.A.P. at Ratsua and to my delight two of the boys I had spoken to back at the barge were already there and safe.

'Later I with others was evacuated back to Torokina in the hospital launch *Stradbroke 11*. It was a beautiful sailing yacht but was the roughest boat ride I ever had, even the sailors were sick. In the Hospital at Torokina I was able to write a letter to my Mother telling her that I was O.K. and she got it before the "We regret to inform......" telegram arrived.

'As soon as I was discharged from Hospital I called at the Boomerang fighter base at Torokina and met the pilot who spotted me in the water and notified the boys at base. I thanked him with all my heartfelt feelings – hope you are still O.K. Bluey. I gave him a couple of bottles of beer which had been issued to me which he appreciated very much.'

'The trauma of my experience played havoc with me for years and at night I still relive the incidents and lucky escapes. This is the first I have ever spoken or written of some of these experiences. It's only the last couple of years that I have not kept away from ex-service events like Reunions, etc., but I am pleased that now the ice is broken I don't feel so bad about it. My mate Welshie is still alive and now I communicate with him often.'

Support Units 15

A dominant theme in the recollections of the elderly survivors was the gratitude they felt for the heroic contribution made by all the support units. The men claimed that the crew of the landing craft, the pilots, the artillery and machine gunners, the engineers and the ambulancemen, the whole united team ensured their successful deliverance from almost certain death at Porton. Support made survival possible in an impossible situation and all units were richly deserving of the men's gratitude.

Lieutenant Graham, R.A.E., described the heroic and indispensable part played by his engineers and men who crewed the assault boats, and Lieutenant Sparks' report confirmed the expertise and accuracy of 4th Field Regt. gunners. The contribution made by landing barges and aircraft was also inspiring beyond measure.

a/ The Barges.

The water transport action at Porton Plantation was known in the 42 Landing Craft Coy as "Operation Porton". According to the O.C. Captain Stuart Leslie it was the most daunting task of the unit's war-time exploits and the casualty rate was very high:

> 'The Northern Detachment of the Company totalled 26 ranks, so we lost half of it – five killed and eight wounded. Our water transport troops performed extremely well in difficult conditions, and it was a tribute to their early training that they

suffered intense enemy fire without flinching.

'It was a very emotional experience to be involved in action so close to the end of the war and to see so many fine soldiers who had been with us for so long killed or wounded. Harry Burrell certainly earned his decoration and, although he was slightly wounded himself, he even personally carried Johnnie Bourke's body ashore after the action.'

The appreciation from Lieutenant Colonel J. Kelly, C.O. of the 31st/51st Australian Infantry Battalion, underscored the crucial role played by water transport in "Operation Porton":

'Much credit for the success of the evacuation is due to the courageous efforts of the Landing Craft Coy in pushing their craft to the beach in the face of heavy fire, and with total disregard for their own safety.'

The Northern Detachment of 42 Landing Craft Company operated from their base on Saposa Island. An important adjunct to the Company was the 1st Australian Water Ambulance Convoy, and 2 barges and 7 crew of that Convoy joined the Detachment at Saposa on June 9 1945. The ambulance barges were LC15s modified to carry 16 stretchers each and, like the others, they doubled as supply barges when necessary.

Evacuation from forward areas was mainly carried out by barge. Depending on the seriousness of the injury, the wounded were taken back to either the Advanced Dressing Station at Ratsua or the recently constructed and appointed

Medical Dressing Station at Soraken where there was a surgeon attached at all times. The yacht *Stradbroke* was responsible for returning seriously wounded troops to the base hospital at Torokina.

AWM Photo 093068. Men wounded at Porton being transferred by barge from the 19 Field Ambulance main dressing station out to The Hospital Ship Stradbroke for the trip to the hospital at Torokina.

Jack Woodman was a coxswain on one of the Water Ambulance barges attached to the 42nd Landing Craft Coy. He explained how he came to be at Porton:

> 'My barge had been supporting the units that were in action in South Bougainville when, early in June '45, I received a message to go to North Bougainville immediately as the 31st/51st had run into trouble. We re-fuelled at Torokina and also took on a load of ammunition for the 4th Field Regiment Artillery. We arrived at Soraken, where

the 25 pounders were operating from, late at night on 9 June. After unloading, Captain Leslie and a native pilot boy called Mauri joined us and we cruised around for several hours, I presume looking for survivors or bodies, before heading to Saposa Island. This was the base where we were to remain until a month after the end of the war.

'We made a daily run over to Ratsua to pick up any wounded who had come in from Porton and transfer them on. As soon as we left Saposa on our trip to Ratsua , Ossie [Tony Ostler] would take the gun covers off and give them a clean all ready for use, but we never had to use them. Each morning we would travel to a two-plank jetty at Ratsua and remain there until a runner would come and inform us if casualties were on the way, or to return to Saposa. Ossie would then put messages on two pigeons telling Field Ambulance at "Freddie" Beach of the type of wounds our patients had.

'We were never told that the Jap positions at Buoi and Porton Plantations were so close. From the jetty a track ran over to the other side of the island to Ruri Bay. There was also the start of the track into Buoi, and the Japs were sending patrols across these tracks daily. This was only a couple of hundred yards from where we were. Our native pilot boy often said "Japan man watching in jungle". It is hard to understand why the Japs did not attack us, just to get hold of a barge in good working order. As most of the barge crews that took part in the landing and evacuation were sent straight back to Torokina, we never heard the true story of the action till some time later.

'The 11th Brigade did have a small rest camp on Soraken and the Japs would shell this beach as soon as they spotted troops swimming. Our course to Ratsua was directly under the shells going over. The Japs would set jam-tin mines overnight so our pilot boy had to remain very alert, and they also used to paddle their canoes into our anchorage of a night and throw phosphorous bombs or grenades into our craft.'

b/ The Pilots.

The pilots flying over Porton during the battle had a "bird's eye view" of the whole sorry saga being played out below them. After leaving their base at Piva North near Torakina, the R.A.A.F. No.5 Squadron Boomerang fighters flew at great risk at treetop level to mark targets for both the Artillery and the R.N.Z.A.F. Corsair bombing operations. The successful evacuation of the assault force from the beach was due largely to the invaluable support given by these aircraft. Their intervention also bought time for the battered troops on stranded barges who waited so long in hope of rescue. Jack Hearn was a No. 5 Squadron Boomerang pilot in the battle at Porton and his memories remain vivid:

'We of course flew right down on the deck at nearly all times and could even see the footprints in the sand. We could generally get a good idea of what was going on. Things were different in those days and we were warned that there was no doubt if you were shot down you would never come out of there alive and we know that for a fact.

Flight-Lieut. Jack Hearn ,No. 5 Army Co operation Squadron R.A.A.F.

'I can remember plainly seeing our AIF boys that had been hit and killed, fallen overboard and grabbed by huge sea-going salt water crocodiles. Flying low down over the reefs, I have had crocodiles snap at the aircraft like a dog would as you passed low over the top of them. Another lad [alive when I saw him last] at this Porton deal had swum some few hundred yards down the coast from the barges and was standing stark naked on the coral some 50 yards offshore, in which area there were large sharks and the crocodiles. I felt very sorry for him as we flew over as there was no way of helping him ....I have carried that image in my mind for 59 years and often wondered what that boy's fate was.' [That "boy" was Viv Taylor and they have now been able to make contact with each other.]

'Somehow or other the Army were able to go in at night and bring out survivors who were brought back to hospital at Torokina. We [5 Squadron] pilots visited them in hospital and they were extremely grateful for the cover we gave them. They were only kids 18 and 19 years old. Of course the New Zealanders did a great job at this time with the dive bombing in this particular event, and many others. It was indeed a good team effort. There wasn't a lot of publicity put about in

> Australia about what happened, but it was a pretty unfortunate incident.'

Among the R.N.Z.A.F. pilots responsible for the airstrikes at Porton was Flying Officer Bryan Cox. He recorded his experiences in a book, *Too Young to Die,* in which he recalls:

> "We had no knowledge of the landing at Porton Plantation until in the afternoon when we were called out in Squadron strength of twelve aircraft to cover the withdrawal of the Australian forces. We approached the Plantation carrying 325 pound depth charges and found the Australian landing barges firmly stuck on a reef, about 200 yards from the Plantation, which consisted of coconut palms. About 150 troops had made the landing the previous morning but by now they had been somewhat reduced in number by the Japanese Imperial Marines stationed in the area, and we could see about fifty soldiers either swimming out to the landing barges, or crouching inside them, or in the water just behind them – with splashes in the water from Japanese fire.
>
> 'We were ordered to bomb the beach front, regardless of how many unfortunate Aussies were still on the shore, then make continuous strafing runs in the usual pairs, running in from the sea towards the land. Why this direction was chosen instead of an attack parallel to the coast I don't know! During these runs only slightly above the landing barge we got a close up view of the poor Aussies crouching in the water and on the barge.

'The aircraft again flew sorties over the area next day to keep down hostile fire as efforts were continued to rescue the stranded troops. Corsairs with a Boomerang lead-in circled over Porton in the afternoon and bombs were dropped very close to the badly-holed barge. Unable to penetrate the heavy curtain of fire, the rescue craft was eventually forced to retire.

'I felt sheer pity for them, thinking thank God I'm not in their position because I could see the way they were crouching and looking at us that they were pretty terrified and so I was certainly pleased I was in the Corsair and not one of them.

'Some 70 hours after the initial landing, in the early hours of 11th June, the last of our troops was rescued. In the morning aircraft searched the area for any survivors. They flew to the north and south of Porton and nearby islands. No sightings were made except for some face down in the sea floating out on the ebb tide. Eight Corsairs made their final sweep over Porton. They bombed the now abandoned barges and strafed the area, with unobserved results.'[64]

[64] *Too Young to Die,* Bryan Cox, Century Hutchinson, Auckland, N.Z.

The Washup 16

The battle of Porton Plantation was a disaster and a tragedy for all concerned. Neither of its objectives was achieved; the Japanese were not forced to withdraw as anticipated, and it was therefore impossible to establish a beachhead on Porton beach. The reasons were that the force attacked with too few craft and too few men for the job, that there was insufficient backup, and serious mistakes were made in the planning of the battle.

Taking into account the historical and political factors leading up to this offensive, the official Intelligence reports and Unit diaries available from that time, and the eye-witness accounts of the men who survived the battle, the conclusions to be drawn are inescapable.

The battle of Porton Plantation, like many others in New Guinea and Bougainville in the concluding days of World War 11, should never have happened. John Hetherington, in *Blamey, Controversial Soldier,* maintains that the over-riding reason for these operations was political, that 'the real purpose was to keep the Australian Army in the field, apparently contributing a worthwhile share towards the defeat of Japan.'[65]Such unnecessary battles, launched by General Sir Thomas Blamey with the approval and support of the government of the day, "had no strategic value in the defeat of the Japanese forces in the S.W. Pacific or in the defence of Australia."[66] It was widely believed that

[65] *Blamey, Controversial Soldier,* John Hetherington, Canberra, 1973.

[66] *The Unnecessary War,* Peter Charlton, Macmillan Australia, 1983, p1

their main objective was the enhancement of Blamey's peacetime career and Australia's post-war prestige in the Pacific. In pursuing this objective it has been documented that 1048 Australian servicemen lost their lives needlessly in ten months in New Guinea and Bougainville.[67]

The planning of the Porton operation was considered by company commanders at the time to be hasty and incompetent. They were also critical of the lack of tactical resources available to them and recommended that the battle should not proceed. Their concerns were: that one company was not sufficient to both hold a beachhead and also press on inland to cause the enemy to withdraw; that intelligence estimates of the numbers, disposition and strength of the opposing force were unreliable; that the promised troop reinforcements were not available and ammunition was in short supply; aerial reconnaissance showed that the coral reef would be extremely dangerous for landing craft but air drops of critical supplies was not considered appropriate by Brigade. Major Dick Sampson, Captain Clyde Downs and Captain Blue Shilton together made these points unequivocally in their reports but were overruled by Brigade.

Unaware of the deficiencies in planning, the 190 battle-weary young men who were sent into Porton became the victims of the incompetence of their military leaders at a high level of command.

They were not prepared for the loss of their heavy weapons and supplies of ammunition on the reef during the landing. In his detailed report Major Sampson referred to the planners' lack of clear identification of the landing site.

[67] *Blamey, Controversial Soldier,* John Hetherington, Canberra, 1973.

This caused the landing to be made at the wrong place and the stores barge to be grounded on the reef with loss of arms and supplies.

Sampson also claimed that the native water transport pilot should have been an inhabitant of Porton with local knowledge of the reef. In addition, the landing was made despite the Landing Craft Company's urgent warning that many of the barges were unserviceable and the reef too hazardous to enter at low tide - which was clear from recent aerial reconnaissance surveys of the area.

The troops were not prepared for the superior numbers and firepower of the enemy. According to Major Sampson's report,

> 'A complete analysis of probable enemy strength was not made......[though] TacR reports indicated work on new positions in the area in addition to several old ones.... the prevailing opinion in high quarters was that all "A" Company would strike would be a few scattered parties of the enemy. This opinion could not have been sustained if the situation and information had been studied thoroughly.'

The men were unprepared for the total failure of backup. This included Brigade's non-delivery of the critical airdrops of ammunition which had been called for frequently by C.O. Captain Downs but which were ignored or refused by Brigade. In addition, apart from one platoon of "C" Company at "Freddie" Beach, there was no reserve of troops for the operation. Stocks of some ammunition were low with insufficient reserve to provide for all possible eventualities. Lieutenant Arthur Graham, C.O. 16 Field Company [R.A.E.] was critical of the timing of the offensive:

> 'The current feeling was that too much haste in planning and preparation was evident. Resources appeared inadequate at a time when there were normal shortages of 5A ammunition and artillery supplies, plus shortcomings on the transport side – mainly by water.'

Lieutenant Blue Reiter was one of the few who were aware of the decision to go in to Porton. It was his opinion that haste should not be seen as a primary cause of the poor planning.

> 'Porton was not a spur-of-the-moment decision as I knew two weeks beforehand that a landing was to be made. However, Artillery were not properly told because, as the O.C. 4th Field Regiment said, he would have built up a supply of ammo instead of having the shortage, and ammo having to be rushed in. R.A.A.F. at Torokina were not notified as, after Porton [at a R.A.A.F. Base dinner] I was told a large number of their planes were being overhauled at that time to be ready for later action.'

Lieutenant Reiter was very cynical about the lack of recognition given to the 31st/51st troops after Porton. Awards which had been highly recommended by Major Sampson and himself were not forthcoming:

> 'Decorations and awards were allotted immediately to Artillery, Landing Craft Company, Transport, Engineers, and [except for Private Ward re smoke canisters] nothing was given to 31st/51st troops on Porton. The cause of this I am led to believe is what Major Sampson, OC Rescue, and

I, Lieutenant Reiter, had put in our reports on Porton. Brigade Staff wanted us to rewrite them, which we refused to do. No doubt the truth hurt, so the recommendations we made were destroyed. General Savige, C.C. Bougainville, told me after the war this was why no awards had been made for 31st/51st troops.

'Being 11th Brigade [not 31st/51st Battalion] I was given the M.C. for Porton and the battle at Sisivie some months before. Two blokes in my platoon were nominated for one – Doug Seymour of Hughenden and Eric Hall.'

Major Dick Sampson was critical of Brigade when his request for an ALCA during the final rescue of the men on the stranded barge was summarily dismissed:

'Those in the rear were only making guesses at the situation and requests from those on the spot should have been granted. By sheer good luck we rescued the remainder but the result had every chance of being different. Interference from the rear came again with a signal for the barge with twelve rescued men on board to return. This was ill-advised as it is most dangerous to have craft on its own amongst the reefs at night.'

The troops on Porton beach were unprepared for Brigade's lack of a contingency plan for evacuation when it became necessary. Major Sampson spoke of this on *The Savage Shore:*

'Well we hadn't prepared for an evacuation at all – we hadn't prepared for losing a hell of a lot of the reserves of ammunition and rations on a barge not

> making it ashore. [We] never practised evacuating a force ever. That was something which just hit us out of the blue.
>
> 'The complete failure of the plan was due mainly to the lack of detailed planning and consideration of the factors involved. Also because the landing took place too soon, before our [other] troops were within striking distance of Porton'.

Captain Blue Shilton was a realist:

> 'So they hadn't done enough homework. The R.A.A.F. intelligence man at the briefing warned of the reefs at the landing area, he warned of the Japanese positions and pillboxes etc., but General Blamey was in the area and I think the Brigade Headquarters and Divisional Headquarters wanted to impress him.'

Significant damage to the force occurred because of Brigade's persistent disregard of warning signals from "A" Company about the situation at Porton. In spite of the caution that the jetty area was dangerously infiladed by the enemy and that the company's ammunition supplies were short, Brigade went ahead with a futile plan to bring in supplies by barge, thus exposing the men and landing craft crews needlessly to heavy Japanese automatic and small arms fire. Because the attempt failed, and because Brigade had disregarded Company's suggestion that an air-drop of supplies would be a practical alternative, the vital ammunition did not reach "A" Company. This non-delivery at a crucial time was to irretrievably jeopardise the outcome of the battle.

According to Signallers at Company Headquarters, on the morning of June 9 there were repeated requests from Captain Downs for immediate and urgent evacuation of his men, especially the wounded, from the beach. This was not achieved until 4.30 p.m. which meant that badly injured men were forced to endure many more hours of exposure to the heat of the tropical sun as well as the constant enemy bombardment.

The T.V. documentary *The Savage Shore* records interesting findings:

> 'By the end of the Bougainville campaign the 31st/51st Battalion would have suffered more battle casualties than any other unit in its Brigade and in its last major action at Porton Plantation one company would be decimated, suffering a casualty rate not seen since Tobruk or Kokoda.'

Lieutenant Blue Reiter observed:

> 'After the Porton show was over, with C.O. Captain Downs missing in action, I was given command of "A" Company with only 19 men on their feet, so had to build it up again.
>
> 'After Porton was over came the worst job. I always hated to sit down to write to the next of-kin of those Killed in Action, and posted Missing. To the wives, mothers and families, I salute you.'

17 Last Words

General Sir Thomas Blamey:

'It was one of the most stirring episodes I have seen. I was deeply impressed by the determined courage of the men. It was a most gallant and inspiring spectacle, and showed in a marked degree, the close co-operation that General Savige had developed with the R.A.A.F. and R.N.Z.A.F.

'The Australian action at Porton Plantation took place over four days, and resulted in the Australians killing an estimated 200 Japanese. It was the scene of many individual acts of heroism when barges in the operation grounded on an uncharted reef.'

Blue Reiter's meeting with General Blamey after Porton sums up in a plain man's words the whole sorry episode:

'After Porton I was to meet Blamey and some of his staff at "Freddie" Beach. He shook hands with me and congratulated me on the job the men had done. It was equal to Gallipoli, France, Tobruk, etc., then he asked me for my opinion of the operation. I stated, "Sir, I joined up in 1939, was in the first Desert show, Greece, Crete, Milne Bay, and stated that on the surrender of Crete I escaped and returned to my unit six months later." I said I had seen some stuff-ups in these places but this was the greatest stuff-up of them all. We talked for a while , he shook hands with me wishing me all the best and left. Brigade Major then put me under open arrest for using insulting language to a superior officer.'

Captain Blue Shilton:

"It is no wonder Porton is not on the map – the services don't like to admit a defeat and certainly not Brigadiers and higher who rely on success for their promotion and only really see the troops as expendable. A bit harsh on my part but six years in the infantry taught me to be realistic. All those men who were sacrificed for no good reason – as Dick Sampson said, we could have continued our steady advance up the coast and achieved the same result with far less casualties. I took 21 plus my batman to Porton – 9 were killed and 7 wounded, a shocking percentage.

'To conclude I think this was a very badly planned operation with no real appreciation of the enemy strength and certainly no thought of the troops' chance of survival. An operation to satisfy higher command and impress General Blamey who was in the area. To hell with the troops!'

Lieutenant Arthur Graham:

'Unlike poet William Wordsworth whose "host of golden daffodils flash upon the inward eye", my "inward eye" sees blood-red poppies as I ponder on the futility of the sad event of the Porton action. This was ennobled only by the magnificent resoluteness of the assaulting and withdrawing troops of 11 Australian Infantry Brigade. Any salute accorded to them must fall far short of what they deserve. No daffodils in victory bouquets – rather the reddest of red poppies equivalent to the red badges of courage they were fully entitled to wear.'

Major Russell Lyons:

'It was the phoniest of phoney wars, a depraved example of man's inhumanity to man, a betrayal of decency and loyalty to pay homage to the empire builders of effete democracy.

'There can be no progress along any road so vile as one which perpetuates human conflict for the aggrandisement and advancement of others who make no sacrifices.'

Peter Charlton:

'It was also a betrayal of faith, the fighting man's faith in his leader's ability and the system which he trusts will bring him home safely when the shooting stops.'

Private Joe Chapel:

'It was all so futile-what a waste!

'THE MAN IN CHARGE DIDN'T CARE!'

After Porton

The 31st/51st Battalion was relieved by the 8th Battalion of the 23rd Brigade on June 28 and returned to Torokina. After peace was declared on August 8 many of the troops faced months of garrison duty in the Occupation Force on Nauru, Ocean Island and New Britain before they were demobilized. The repatriation of Japanese prisoners of war from these places took place between February 28 and March 6 1946.

Major W. Hughes records in the history of the 31st/51st Battalion:

> 'In October 1945 at the cessation of hostilities a reconnaissance party which included Major Dick Sampson and Lieutenants Blue Reiter and Edgar Ebsary, returned to the Porton battlefield. To their surprise they found that the Japanese buried the Australian dead and erected a [crude] memorial which when translated read, "The Australian soldiers buried here died by the sea."
>
> 'The Japanese however, did not bury many of their dead, as Lieutenant Blue Reiter states that around the Australian perimeter were at least fifty badly decayed enemy corpses, some still with their rifles and equipment. These, and the unknown number of dead that were recovered during the battle, as was their practice, indicates that a great many of them had been killed and wounded.
>
> 'The two barges left at Porton after the battle are still there, as confirmed in a recent photo from Lieutenant Mashhiro Kurimato, a veteran of the

Bonis Peninsula campaign. All the plantations on Bonis Peninsula and at Soraken Plantation are now deserted and all buildings have been destroyed by fire, by the Bougainville separationist movement.

'After the war, Porton Plantation was owned by the descendants of Robert Pitt, a well known Coast Watcher on the island during the Japanese occupation of the island. The Soraken Plantation was later owned by New Guinea Plantation Pty. Ltd. and was managed by Roger Gillbanks.

'Sometime in 1986, John Feltham visited Porton and observed the two barges on the reef. The anti-tank gun which was on the stores barge is easily seen in the crystal clear water. How it got there is not known.

'During a reconnaissance of the area beyond Porton, Feltham's party located a crashed R.N.Z.A.F. Corsair in the area. The pilot, fully kitted, was still in the cockpit. He was identified by the ring on the finger of his skeletal remains as Flying Officer B.T. Clark.'[68]

Sergeant Norm Strange, M.M., E.D., was a platoon leader in the 8th Battalion which relieved the 31st/51st Battalion after Porton. Shortly after the war ended he volunteered to go back to Bougainville with the War Graves team. He has grim memories of this experience:

'We found 62 bodies [on Bougainville] which

[68] *At War with the 31/51st Infantry Battalion,* Major W.E.Hughes MBE RL, Church Archivist Press, 1993, p252.

are now in the cemetery at Port Moresby. It had been arranged that a party of Japanese would meet us at Ratsua to guide us to the bodies of Australians who were buried, at the war's end, in Japanese territory just south of Porton.

'This was an unpleasant task but it was satisfying to know that they would be buried in a proper War Cemetery. At Porton we only found one grave with no name.'

Porton Beach

Porton Beach

Extract from Tommy Rose's Letter to his Wife. Sept. 1945

'A few of us with Lieut. Jackson set off in a launch for Porton Beach to try and find Bob Kennon's body. Eight miles up the coast we went straight to the place where I last saw Bob. Sure enough there were his remains in a hole in the coral in less than three feet of water. We got everything that belonged to him even his identification tags. Wasn't that wonderful after the poor kid had been there in the water for over three months?

We brought him back to camp and fixed things up and he was buried later on in the day. They gave him a wonderful service, I'll never forget it. Six of us formed a guard and carried him etc. The Padre brought a huge bunch of beautiful pink lilies picked fresh from the jungle and Bob was buried as he would have wanted it alongside his mates.

Hell he was a good kid Ida, they don't come any better or gamer than Bob Kennon. Won't it be wonderful for his people to know his body has been found as they were first notified that he was missing, and then believed killed, now they will be able to get a photograph of his grave etc. and know that at least he did get a decent burial.

Perhaps some day the story of the evacuation from Porton Beach will be told, but I doubt it as the whole thing was such a terrific muddle it is best if they forgot it ever happened.'

Epilogue

The Pilgrimage:

Alone on Porton beach in December 2002 I held in my hand a rough sketch of the battlefield, drawn by Blue Reiter at my request.

After initial difficulties were overcome and some confusion as to the location of Porton Plantation was sorted out, this visit had been made possible through the generous assistance of The Defence Department and the Department of Veteran Affairs. Bougainville was still regarded as dangerous after the island's ten years of civil war, and I was placed under the protection of the Buka Peace Monitoring Group during my short stay. These were competent and caring people and I cannot praise them highly enough.

Porton was a lonely and abandoned place. There was no name to be seen, no monument or plaque, nothing at all to identify this battlefield for the loved ones of the men who fought and died here.

The beach was already hot at 9 a.m. Radiating off the loose white sand the heat brushed my face in little eddies and thrust through the soles of my light sneakers. Behind me, rising above the tangled undergrowth, Porton Plantation's once-orderly rows of coconut palms marched eastwards in close formation to meet the distant dark wall of the jungle.

In front of me lay the glittering blue world of the Pacific Ocean, cobalt in the deep water of the channels, opalescent inshore among the reefs. On a western aspect of the reef about 150 metres from the beach a faint dark smudge indicated the remains of the wrecked landing craft, ALCA 213. This was the object of my visit, the place where my father lost his life in 1945. A mantle of stillness and tropical languor hung softly over the bright sea and the verdant shore. Porton in 2002, though lonely, was hushed and serenely beautiful in its solitude.

It was impossible to imagine how different this quiet, secluded place must have looked in 1945. Using Blue's sketch I made rough guesses about the organization of the beachhead area at that time, the position of the platoons and weapon pits. The site of the water hole and the contested jetty and landing areas were clearly marked on his diagram which also showed the daunting proliferation of Japanese pill-boxes and trenches encircling the beach, a deadly trap for the unwary.

However it was not until two years later when I read the detailed accounts of Porton survivors that I was able to associate those stories with the beach on which I had been standing in 2002. I could visualize then the determination of the troops who had waded ashore at that spot in 1945, dug weapon pits and gone on to fight against impossible odds even after all hope seemed lost. My thoughts were of the courage of the daring rescuers who returned time after time through the dangerous reefs to save their wounded and trapped mates. Many lost their own lives during those attempts.

From the survivors' stories I became aware of the unrelieved horror that my father shared with these men. I tried to imagine their frustration and powerlessness as they were confined in pits or incarcerated on sinking barges in the bloodied sea. I thought of the powerlessness of commanders whose warnings had been ignored; they watched the assault falling apart around them, as they knew it would, and were now helpless to prevent the disaster or save their men.

But foremost in my mind was the leader of the assault force, the C.O. whose men claimed that they were like family and were always his first consideration. The Skipper whose repeated and urgent requests for ammunition airdrops to resupply his men now in imminent danger of being overrun by the enemy were ignored or rejected by higher authority at a safe distance from the action. I thought mostly about the C.O. Captain Clyde Downs, my cherished father, who was one of the many victims of the deadly Porton fiasco. I learned from the men's stories, for the first time, that he had been wounded at Porton – the second time possibly fatally.

Back on Porton beach in 2002, now accompanied by one of the Peace Monitors, I waded out to the remains of ALCA 213 on the reef. Unlike the troops in '45 I carried no weapons, no pack, only a simple wreath of flowers which I attached to that tragic wreck in memory of my father. I spent some minutes there with my thoughts. Along with abiding sadness was also a feeling of bitterness at his cruel and unnecessary death - emotions shared by the loved ones of all those who died at Porton.

After leaving the barge I walked to the area of the destroyed jetty and waded into the sea again for about 100 metres. There I gently floated another wreath of flowers in the clear blue water to honour all the indomitable men of Porton who had fought here so bravely and so loyally, in the true spirit of Anzac.

While we stood on the beach watching the flowers being carried out to sea the Peace Monitors joined us and together we recited the Ode of Remembrance – lest we forget. The survivors have never forgotten.

After returning from Bougainville I wrote to Ms Dana Vale, Minister for Veteran Affairs in 2002, to request on behalf of the Porton veterans and their families that a permanent memorial be erected on Porton beach to commemorate this battle and identify the battlefield for future pilgrims. The Minister declined my request. As political unrest persisted in Bougainville and the Australian Peace Monitoring Group was soon to be removed her decision was understandable but disappointing.

In the crucible of Porton, June 1945, was forged a bond of mateship which has over the years proved indestructible and infinitely more precious than the purest gold. Porton is those men's story, it belongs to every one of them. As the daughter of Clyde Downs I am privileged to have helped them tell it.

Author on Porton Beach

Post Script

In 1945, having escaped the hellfire of Porton where they saw their mates falling on every side from enemy bullets, the survivors must have believed themselves to be indestructible. In 1946 they bravely accepted the challenges of peace-time Australia and committed themselves to the future in a society which was still reeling from the impact of six years of war and brief enemy invasion from the air at Darwin and Townsville. The diggers whose stories have appeared in this book took up varied careers after their discharge from the armed forces.

Ron Codrington briefly became an orchardist and then went into the motor industry. He married and after several years as manager for Angaston Motors he moved to Adelaide and joined Toyota. Here he became Settlement Officer of the commercial division before retiring at 58. In good health and with two new hips, Ron is a keen bowler who travels to the Gold Coast every year to compete, 'with some success.'

> 'After Porton I always thought every day a bonus.'

Stiffy Flynn settled in Townsville after being discharged. Here he worked first at R.A.A.F. Headquarters and then at the Government Tourist Bureau as a travel consultant. He retired in 1983, enjoys good health and is now 'mainly employed as a 'Spanish gardener' – manual labour – for my good wife, Pat.'

'**John Goodchild**, back in the everyday world, found employment with a large machinery company as a field sales representative. He took up his studies again where he had left off on enlisting, and completed a Graduate Diploma in Engineering. After five years with the Dept. of Harbours and Marine he and his family moved to the central west of Queensland for health reasons. After twenty-five years in and around western areas he retired to Toowoomba in 1980.

> "One enduring memory I have of my (army) service is of the friendships formed in those times, which have lasted throughout the years." [69]

Eric Hall returned to his home town of South Johnstone after his discharge and rejoined the National Bank at Innisfail. Married, and with a family, he worked at eleven National Bank Branches throughout the state and in some or all places was actively associated with RSL, Rugby League, tennis, cricket, bowls, Rotary, Show, Races, school and Church. At Tara he was honoured with life membership of the RSL for services over the years. After retiring in 1982 to the Redcliffe Peninsular Eric has had six heart bypass operations.

> 'Now, going on for 82 I am starting to feel the strain and as they say, 'que sera, sera.' Whatever will be will be. It reminds me of sitting in the boat at Porton.'

Blue Reiter was not demobilized until February 1946 having been given the task of escorting Japanese prisoners of war from Nauru and Ocean Island back to Torokina.

[69] *Lives and Times,* Ed. John Gardner.

He then spent two months in hospital nursed by the young woman he was to marry.

Blue bought a 124 - acre dairy farm in Victoria as part of the Government-sponsored soldier settlement scheme. With much hard work and modern innovations and fertilizers, production increased 800% and his herd from 30 to 120 cows. He won the Victorian Dairy Farmer of the Year Award in 1964, bought another farm and a beef bull, and he and his family prospered from that time onward, 'the best years of my life'.

After selling the farm in the 1970s and taking up their hobby of gem stone mining in N.S.W. and western Queensland, Blue and his wife retired in 1979 to Nambour in Queensland. They continued their visits to the gem fields for another ten years until Blue's wife died and his old war injuries prevented him mining.

Maintaining a keen interest in Australian army history and his war-time unit Blue keeps close contact with his Porton mates and is seen every Anzac Day "marching" in his wheelchair in front of the $31^{st}/51^{st}$ Battalion banner. The crowd loves him.

Blue Reiter and Stuart Leslie, Mooloolaba 2005

Dick Sampson returned to work after WWII in the Commonwealth Bank and studied Economics at the University of Sydney. In 1956 he became one of the founding members of the Reserve Bank of Australia. He was seconded to the Bank of England in 1960 to further his

Dick Sampson

knowledge of the management of national debt. His expertise in central banking then took him to Zambia [previously Northern Rhodesia] as Deputy Governor of the Bank of Zambia in 1965.

Returning to Australia in 1968 he was the representative for Australia on various central banking courses around the world but particularly in Asia. He retired from the Reserve Bank in 1976 to make clocks and play golf.

Blue Shilton, married and with a family, in November 1945 rejoined the stockbroking firm he had worked with pre-war. Although he worked long hours and was plagued by recurrent attacks of malaria he achieved notable success in the years which followed. However, the fifteen-hour days, seven days a week, and worsening malaria led to his physical breakdown in 1948.

By 1949 Blue had recovered and commenced operating on the trading floor of the Melbourne Stock Exchange which he continued to do for 21 years. Coping competently with the fall-out from the mining boom and bust of the 1960s and 70s, Blue gained seniority and became the managing partner in his company until he retired in 1979.

He then became a profitable "Collins St. farmer" for 20 years and invested in rural property.

Older and a bit frail now, Blue and his wife take life very quietly. Their son warns him, "you're in the frame Dad."

Viv Taylor put the army behind him in 1945. He received Post War Reconstruction training in the building trade at Stafford in Brisbane in the 1950s.

Becoming a plasterer, he then worked in western Queensland

Viv Taylor

as a contractor in the 1960s. Married, with a family, Viv then bought a small business in Nambour which was the first of a number of successful small business enterprises which followed, building on his success with each change.

He retired in 1974 and spent several years travelling around Australia though his base remained in Nambour. Here he joined the Lions Club and became involved in many local community projects. In general good health, he keeps in close touch with his old Army mate 'Welshie' (Dick Welsh).

Jack Woodman returned to Melbourne after his discharge to finish his plumbing apprenticeship and in due course started his own business at Albury.

> "Following the death of my wife in 2000, I now live a quiet existence, playing cards, gardening and writing to my old army mates. The one I miss most is Don Kennedy although I'd have to read his letters six times to understand the writing!"

Jack's family co-sponsors the "John Woodman Memorial Bike Race", named after Jack's son, killed while training at the age of 31. He has been involved inMeals-on-Wheels for 40 years, is a Rotarian and Legacy member, and a keen supporter of the Sydney Swans.

Felix Grasso

After war ended and Felix had recouperated from his wounds, he returned to Babinda where he had cut cane before enlisting and married Anna Fracchia in October 1946. They had two daughters, Linda and Sylvia.

Due to his injuries, Felix was unable to return cutting to

Felix Grasso

cane, so he and Anna moved to Cairns where he worked for Main Roads Department for a period. He then became Supervisor for the Migrant Centre in Cairns, where he helped displaced persons coming from Europe, to find work on the canefields in and around Cairns.

In the early fifties the Migrant Centre closed and Felix went to work for A.J. Drapers selling real estate. Due to the closure of this business and the eventual sale of the freehold of this property, Felix commenced his own Agency, first operating out of our family home and then from it's present site. Felix continued to operate the business together with Anna for approx. 20 years prior to retiring due to ill health. Felix passed away at the age of 82 on the 23/12/2000.

Stuart Leslie was demobilized in April 1946, rejoined the Insurance Company he was with pre-war, and became an active member of the Liberal party. He married and had a family in the following years.

Setting up his own Insurance brokerage led Stuart to an affiliation with Lloyds of London and an international career which spanned thirty years and many countries.

After retiring he then devoted his time to the Winston Churchill Memorial Trust and the National Heart Foundation for which he was awarded the Order of Australia as a member, AM in 1988. Stuart and his wife divided their retirement years between Melbourne and Barwon Heads.

Stuart Leslie

Sadly, Stuart passed away in November, 2005.

Abbreviations

Arty	Artillery
A.A.S.C.	Australian Army Service Corps
2I/C	Second in Command
.3 S&W	Smith and Wesson (pistol)
ALCA	Australian Landing Craft Assault
Bn	Battalion
CO	Commanding Officer
CMF	Citizen Military Forces (Militia)
DSO	Distinguished Service Order
FOO	Forward Observation Officer
JUKI	Japanese Machine Gun
LC 15	Landing Craft 15
LMG	Light Machine Gun
M.B.E.	Member of the British Empire
MM	Military Medal
MC	Military Cross
MIA	Missing in Action
MID	Mentioned in Despatches
MMG	Medium Machine Gun
MO	Medical Officer
NCO	Non Commissioned Officer
OC	Officer Commanding
OP	Observation Post
RAP	Regimental Aid Post
Sig/Sigs	Signals/Signallers
TacR/TacHQ	Tactical Reconnaissance/Tactical Headquarters.

Appendix

A letter fom Sub.Lt. Genna Katsumata who participated in the battle of Porton, to John Feltham of Townsville, reads:

February 18, 1986

Dear All the Brave ex Soldiers Concerned,

This is s great and pleasant surprise to receive your letter of inquiry about us, the survivors of Porton. Above all things, we really feel very glad that it was given to us and unexpected opportunity to show our hearty respect to all the men who attempted the landing on the beach at Porton, on the northern shoreline of Bougainville Island, on June 8th, 1945.

Since this happened the "Do or Die" battle between and us, forty years have passed and things have completely changed, though we still have a vivid recollection of what we did and what we saw then. We are sure that all of you do so too.

Now we think it happy wholeheartedly to inform you of a meeting we have here in Yonago City, along the coast of Japan Sea, in commemoration of the very day, Feb 18, 1946, when we were demobilised. We stepped back into Japan after the long merciless struggle we shared in the battle of hell with the jungle.

To think back over our life on the island those days we all had, in a way, "beyond-description-like" hard times not only fighting against the men but mostly going through all kinds of hardships, particularly such as "vicious" tropical diseases and malnutrition, much more dreadful than bullets, from which we suffered most. The awful shortage of medicine, no regular food but coconuts! In fact, it is no exaggeration to say that almost all of our time was spent hunting anything edible and moreover battling against our thoughts. Who saved our lives God only knows?

Fortunately, these days the relationship between Australia and Japan has increasingly been improved and in those forty years, we believe, have created a new world for us who were once in the same boat. "Yesterday's enemy is today's friend" is indeed, something that can be accepted.

Forty long years! We have aged and still getting older, just like you, though a possible world wide peace must be maintained especially by us, the war-experienced, as long as their exists human beings all over the earth.

We sincerely hope to build a stronger mutual understanding, and try hard to make good friends with each other by means of communications.

Lastly we say to you all, "May the departed on the beach at Porton rest in peace forever!" No more young lives to be wasted in the jungle, we do pray. Good luck to you all!

sincerely yours

Gemma Katsumata

Ex Naval Sub-Lieutenant"

Bibliography

Charlton, Peter *The Unnecessary War*, Macmillan Australia Pty. Ltd., 1983

Cochrane, Peter *Australians at War,* ABC Books, 2001

Cox, Bryan *Too Young to Die,* Century Hutchinson, Auckland, N.Z.1976

Grey, Jeffrey *The Australian Army*, O.U.P., 2001

Hetherington, John *Blamey, Controversial Soldier,* Canberra 1973

Horner, David *Blamey: The Commander-in-Chief,* Allen & Unwin, *1998*

Hughes, Major W.E. *At War with the 51st Infantry Battalion and 31st Infantry Battalion from 1940 to 1946*
Church Archivist Press, Toowoomba, 1993.

Long, Gavin *Australia in the War of 1939-1945. Volume VII The Final Campaigns,* Canberra A.W.M.

McNab, Alexander *We Were the First,* Australian Military History Publications, 1998.

Rice, W.ed. *Sailors in Slouch Hats,* Hesperian Press Victoria Park

Swain, Bruce *A Chronology of Australian Armed Forces at War*, Allenand Unwin, 2001.

Articles:

Rentz, Major John N. *Bougainville and the Northern Solomons* Historical Section , Division of Public Information, U.S. Marine Corps, 1948

NOMINAL ROLL OF PERSONNEL IN HOSPITAL

A COY

QX 39378	CPL	KENRICK	A.C.	
QX 57886	PTE	ASHE	J.P.	w
Q 127855	PTE	KEEGAN	B.R.F.	w
Q 39609	PTE	ABERCROMBIE	T.	
N 238183	PTE	YOUNG	E.	w
QX 33570	SGT	KERNS	W.R.	w
Q 38949	PTE	BAK	L.R.	
QX 42952	SGT	THIEME	G.	
NX 135627	L/CPL.	LANE.	J.	w
NX 187235	PTE	GASH	M.R.	w
VX 65304	PTE	WADE.	J.E.	w
QX 25191	CPL	ANDERSON	J.A.E.	w
QX 56527	PTE	SNELL	G.J.	w
NX 194191	PTE	DOWLING	R.W.	w
QX 49842	A/CPL.	WALSH	R.O.	w
Q 28374	PTE	STEWART	L.D.	w
Q 135452	PTE	JENSEN	T.E.	
N 241926	PTE	GRAINGER	E.K.	w
NX 194197	A/CPL.	CUMBERLAND	A.V.	w
SX 30748	PTE	DUNN	L.H.	w
N 479034	PTE	GRIFFIN	C.H.	w
SX 31262	PTE	CODRINGTON	R.W.	
NX 167245	PTE	McLEAN	J.C.	w
S 39100	PTE	MILLER	H.E.	w
SX 31427	PTE	KEATLEY	N.W.	w
QX 47586	L/CPL.	ROLLEY	H.G.	
NX 153042	PTE	RIGBY	A.J.	w
Q 199488	PTE	FLYNN	L.G.	w
SX 39251	L/CPL.	SCHILLER	B.G.	w
VX 136692	PTE	RYAN	A.C.	w
VX 139051	PTE	PEERS	J.P.	
NX 201839	PTE	SHEARER	W.G.	w
VX 93645	PTE	FRY	R.S.	w
VX 117778	CPL	CAMERON	A.	
NX 156085	PTE	COOPER	C.	w
SX 37276	PTE	NASH	W.E.	w
Q 127856	PTE	KEEGAN	J.R.R.	w
Q 109523	PTE	PURTELL	J.	w
NX 135584	PTE	O'NEILL	C.E.	w
QX 46767	CPL	HALL	E.D.	w
QX 42063	L/SGT	TICKLE	G.H.	w
TX 15135	PTE	DOLAN	R.J.	
SX 19706	PTE	DOLMAN	D.C.	w
QX 56107	PTE	GOODCHILD	J.	w
VX 93593	PTE	PORTER	C.M.	
SX 31263	CPL	WESTLEY	W.J.	w

BN HQ.

W 53810	PTE	CRAWFORD	W.J.
QX 47243	CPL	LYNCH	F.C.

HQ. COY.

SIGS.	QX 33554	PTE.	BRADFORD	E.R.

MMGs.	QX 34018	LT.	PONT	H.	w
	QX 54084	SGT	BRACKLEY	T.	w
	QX 55304	PTE	ABEL	J.S.C.	w
	QX 54785	L/CPL	GRASSO	F.	w
MORs.	QX 37291	PTE	O'DONOHUE	K.J.	w
	QX 53100	PTE	ASPINALL	J.W.	w
	QX 41379	PTE	JARMAN	D.W.	w
	Q 115967	PTE	STAMP	F.L.	w
T/AK	QX 46733	SGT	SHEPHERD	A	w
	QX 44437	PTE	HARDING-WILSON	W.F.	w
	QX 47393	L/CPL	LEPINATH	J.	

C.COY

VX 3379	CAPT	SHILTON	A.L.	w
QX 34012	LT	GILLMAN	N.J.	w
Q 34014	PTE	MYTTON	D.G.	w
Q 39436	PTE	BRADY	F.P.	w
NX 202411	PTE	BURNS	L.S.L.	w
QX 29094	PTE	GRAY	W.L.	
SX 37220	PTE	BARRON	E.	w
V 515879	PTE	MARTIN	R.J.	w
VX 181890	CPL	ANCHEN	A.P.	w
QX 56057	PTE	SPENCER	C.	w
Q 115909	PTE	PITCHER	L.V.	w
N 465963	PTE	BOURKE	F.W.	w

223 SUPPLY DEPOT PL

VX 107817	LT	SCOBIE	K.W.	w
VX 41028	PTE	JENNINGS	H.A.	w
VX 123433	PTE	GLENISTER	R.V.	w
VX 73007	PTE	WILLIAMSON	R.T.	
VX 149977	PTE	MORRISON	A.J.	w
VX 117462	PTE	HARRISON	P.L.	w

4 AUST FD REGT.

VX 69608	SGT	PIERCE	J.L.
WX 25292	BDR	LAMB	R.B.
VX 73295	GNR	GLARE	B.W.
N 203713	GNR	REID	G.
N 442475	GNR	GRAHAM	F.G.

19 AUST FD AMB.

QX 60942	CAPT	MONAGHAN	P.J.
QX 43141	CPL	STRATFORD	J.
QX 51547	CPL	WEST	T.H.
S 114419	PTE	FORNER	A.
NX 163916	PTE	McNALLY	P.
QX 51747	PTE	MITCHELL	C.T.
QX 56224	PTE	TAYLOR	V.H.
V 503005	PTE	WILLIAMS	J.M.

16 AUST FD COY RAE.

QX 40915	L/CPL.	CHAPEL	J.V.	
QX 57488	PTE	KINNE	H.J.	
QX 57449	SPR	KEYWORTH	R.E.	
QX 25165	SPR	ROYAL	T.J.	
Q 76391	SPR	THOMSON	N.J.	
N 223825	SPR	SELLARS	N.E.	
QX 36210	LT	GRAHAM	A.G.	w
QX 40914	CPL	DRAPER	M.L.W.	w

(wounded in evacuation party)

11 BDE SIG SECT.

Q 111979	SIG	BAHR	A.H.
NX 125551	SIG	BURGESS	F.C.
SX 19800	SIG	MOYSE	F.A.

42 LANDING CRAFT COY R.A.E.

VX 61427	SGT	TRAINOR	O.R.	w
VX 103870	CPL	BALL	R.J.R.	w
VX 72107	SPR	NEWTON	H.V.	w
VX 145740	SPR	GOULDING	L	w
VX 61052	SPR	WHELAN	J.J.	w
NX147630	SPR	GRAHAM	A.	w
VX 59659	SPR	BURRELL	H.	w

HONOURS AND AWARDS

MILITARY CROSS

QX36201 Lieutenant Arthur Green Graham of 16 Field Company

VX 40024 Lieutenant Frank Arthur Reiter, 11th Brigade

MILITARY MEDAL

QX 40914 Cpl M.L.W. Draper of 16 Field Company

QX 36212 Staff Sergeant G.P. Blondell of 16 Field Company

VX 59659 Sapper H. Burrell of 42 Landing Craft Coy R.A.E.

VX 94650 Pte. A.P. Olson, "A" Coy 31/51 Aust Inf Bn (AIF)

DISTINGUISHED CONDUCT MEDAL

WX 22431 Pte. K.R. Ward, "A" Coy 31/51 Aust Inf Bn (AIF)

MENTIONED IN DESPATCHES

QX. 40913 Sapper W.F. Dossetto of 16 Field Company R.A.E.

QX. 40913 Sapper G.L. Halford of 16 Field Company R.A.E.

QX. 40913 Sapper C.E. Owen of 16 Field Company R.A.E.

ASSAULT LANDING AT PORTON NORTH BOUGAINVILLE

BY 31/51 AUST INF BN (AIF)

WITH SUPPORTING UNITS

42 AUST LANDING CRAFT COY RAE (AIF)

19 AUST FIELD AMBULANCE (AIF)

16 AUST FIELD COY RAE (AIF)

4 AUST FIELD REGT. RAA (AIF)

223 AUST DEPOT SUPPLY PL

8, 9, 10, 11, 12 JUNE 1945

IN MEMORIAM

31/51 AUST INF BTN (AIF)
A COY

QX 33838 Capt. Downs H.C.
NX 14999 Lt. Smith N.J.
Q 145 277 Pte. Palmer C.A.
NX 154896 L.Cpl. Dinsdale N.
NX 178967 Pte. Salmon J.E.
NX 179453 Pte. Duck E.N.
NX 173969 Pte. Conroy P.L.
Q 122963 Pte. Scriven A.M.
QX 52257 Pte. Burke L.O.D.

C COY

SX 19850 Pte. Leicester K.A.
SX 38799 L.Cpl. Launer L.J.
SX 38800 Pte. Kluski C.S.
VX 131329 Pte. Westcott C.W.J.
S 110375 Pte. Tonkin C.R.
NX 175770 Pte. Haydon H.L.
SX 39054 Pte. Scott W.J.

H.Q. COY

Q 34162 Pte. Keller H.J.

42 AUST. WATER LANDING CRAFT COY RAE (AIF)

VX 60318 Cpl. Burke J.R.
VX 77686 Spr. Kennon R.C.
VX 59160 Spr. Roy G.
VX 60412 Spr. Johnston S.D.
QX 51677 Spr. Kingston T.K.

19 AUST. FIELD AMBULANCE (AIF)

NX 194999 Sgt. Boon J.R.
NX 163756Pte. W.C. Whittington
Q 33995 Pte. Bailey F.A.

16 AUST. FIELD COY. RAE, (AIF)

VX 121252 Spr. Newton A.J.

4AUST. FIELD REGT. (AIF)

Q 267070 Gnr. Payne H.B.

A further 69 of the assault group were wounded in action of a total 107 hospitalized.

APRIL 25

Yes, I am an Australian, today's April 25
A single day within a year of 365
A single day for memories of those dead and alive
A single day for soldiers, and battles revived.

A single day of heroes, as most of them were
The soldiers, the sailors, the men of the air
And all of the doctors and nurses and staff
This day is for them as they all took their part.

The men and the women of two great world wars
Have furnished the backbone from which our strength pours
And our forces who since have honoured the cause
To all I say "Thank You", to you and to yours.

Graham Hall
© 25-4-'85

Son of Eric Hall

Porton Memorial on The Strand Townsville, unveiled August 14th 2005 at VP60 celebrations.

About the Author

Audrey Davidson was born in Malanda on the Atherton Tableland in 1931 and was educated at various schools around Queensland, finishing her secondary studies at Glennie Memorial School, Toowoomba. In the war years the Army posted her father to military training camps at many different Queensland locations and his family followed wherever possible. Capt. Clyde Downs was killed in action in Bougainville in 1945.

After completing her nursing training at the Brisbane General Hospital (now RBH) in 1954 she married and with her husband spent the next ten years living in the United Kingdom and in Ghana and Sierra Leone (West Africa) before returning to Australia.

Taking up external studies again in later years the author graduated from the University of New England, Armidale, with a B.A. in 1994 and a Master of Literature in 1996. In 2002 she made a lone pilgrimage to the battlefield in Bougainville where her father died and, after her research revealed that the tragic conflict was both unnecessary and never fully disclosed, decided to tell the story of the battle of Porton Plantation.

Porton A Deadly Trap is her first book. It took two years to research and write. The first edition was published in 2005 and updated in 2006.

Audrey Davidson and her husband now live in rural retirement in the Gold Coast hinterland and both share a keen interest in military history and the fortunes of the remaining men of the battle of Porton Plantation.